A Priest's Memoir

Living in God's Love with Christ Jesus

As the Father Loves Me, So Do I Love You

As I Love You, So You Must Love One Another

Reverend James H. Short

Barrie Elizabeth Messinger

A Priest's Memoir

Living in God's Love with Christ Jesus

Copyright © 2024 by Tracey M. Downey

Published by: ACH Publishing
www.Achpublishing.com

To the best of my ability, I have re-created events, locales, people, and organizations from my memories of them. In order to maintain the anonymity of others, in some instances I have changed the names of individuals.

Contributors

Barbara, my wife

Pamela Van Natta

Reverend Sandy Blake

Robyn Mitchell
Ryan Short

Clare Harbin

Prologue

This is a story of how God has worked in my life.

There are instances in our lives that have a profound effect on us. Once we are marked as Christ's own forever, He can use our lives for His glory.

What I want to convey is how God has impacted our lives. Everyone has a story. When we did retreats in the mountains when I was at Church of the Ascension, I would have each person start by telling the story of his or her life. When you can bring that story into the light with belief in God's presence and His involvement in our lives, it can have a powerful effect.

Not everyone is baptized, and some have to be inspired to join God in a conscious way.

Paul says, "In Him we live, and move, and have our very existence." More than God being in us, we are in Him. For the baptized person, we are in God's dimension. That is the basis for our faith and our continually turning to Him; it is because He has marked us as His own in Jesus. The Lord said, "On that day you will know that I am in you and you are in me." God's commitment to us is for eternity. He wants us with Him forever.

Jeremiah had a revelation from God: "I have loved you with an everlasting Love, and now in my tender mercy, I draw you to myself." That has been a hallmark in my life, and when I die, I want to ride in on God's tender mercy, not anything I've done or achieved.

What I want to share in the account of my life is to acknowledge and see the places where God has intervened. I want to demonstrate that throughout my life—in my family, in my growing up in my childhood parish, Holy Innocents, and later in my ministry—that God is present in our lives, bidden or not bidden.

My desire is to help people catch hold of the faith they were born into, or if they don't have an active faith, to make a choice to believe.

St. John's Gospel is a foundational source of faith for me, and I can still read it and be inspired by Jesus' kindness, His strength, mercy, and even His boldness in facing the Pharisees and Sadducees.

In 2 Corinthians 5, we are told to be ambassadors of God's reconciliation to each and every one of us, and by implication, to reconcile to one another. Reconciliation is what Jesus was offering when He appeared to the apostles after His crucifixion. He announced Shalom to the apostles, which is the word for healing and reconciling peace. Jesus said, "My Father works even unto now, and I work." The job of the Christian is to be the extension of Jesus to the world. That is what I have tried to live and what I aim to share.

TABLE OF CONTENTS

An Uncertain Beginning

Was I to survive? Would my mother live?

On March 31, 1933, my mother, nine months pregnant, was hemorrhaging and was rushed to the hospital in an ambulance. When my father arrived, the doctor asked him, "Who do you want me to save, your wife or the baby?" My dad immediately replied, "By all means, save my wife!" When you consider that there were four children at home who needed their mother, his answer is understandable.

My aunts, my mother's sisters, were great intercessors, and they began to pray when my mother left for the hospital.

But I lived, and my mother lived. I was born at 11:55 that night. It was a very stressful birth; I must have been a little bent out of shape because my dad said I wasn't a pretty baby. I say, "God wanted us to live!"

A year later as a one-year-old, I was in the hospital with pneumonia. A nurse at the hospital, Mary O'Connor, a young woman from our street, felt prompted to go up to the infant ward to look in on me. She found me blue and not breathing. She picked me up and ministered to me until I started to breathe. Evidently, I was a candidate for SIDS—Sudden Infant Death Syndrome. It was the second time in my short life that I had been saved. God indeed wanted me to live.

At important junctures in my life, God has always intervened to help me do and be what He wants me to be.

The Loss of My Sister

Leading up to my hospitalization with pneumonia, my sister Jeanne's twin, Joan, died at the age of 4½ after a misdiagnosis by the family doctor, who was treating the pains in her stomach as a stomach bug. Her appendix burst, and peritonitis had spread throughout her whole body. Joan cried, and cried and Jeanne, her twin sister, cried along with her. When Joan died, Jeanne immediately fell asleep.

My parents had a burial service for Joan at our parish church, Holy Innocentsce, and the priest dressed in white vestments, which was common for a burial service for babies and small children; it was called the Mass of the Angels.

Jeanne continued to grieve the loss of her twin. She would go to the kitchen to get a cookie and return with a second one for Joan. That would break up the family.

I don't have clear memories of Jeanne until I got older, around age four. Jeanne and I weren't close. She didn't like to read to me, and she didn't like me to sleep next to her. She would get annoyed if I touched her.

My mother grieved and grieved for a year after Joan died. She didn't nurse me for very long; I was bottle-fed early on because I was lactose intolerant. I was a fussy baby. She told me later in life that she worried she didn't care for me very well during that time of grieving. She would change my diaper and then put me down; she didn't hold and cuddle me much, but my father and siblings did. I was too young to remember, but I absorbed a lot of the grief. In addition to my mother being sad, she was asthmatic. I must have been four or five, sitting beside her on the couch in the living room when she was crying. I said, "Mummy, why are you crying?" As the tears flowed down her face, she replied, "I'm thinking of Joan." At one point, my father told her, "Bes, if you don't take hold of your grief, it is going to kill us both."

Aunt Adelaide suggested that my mother start turning toward the Sacred Heart of Jesus. The first Friday of each month, there was a Mass as a devotion to the Heart of Christ, and she would take me to church with her. Aunt Adelaide would go along with us; she was a great strength for my mom and was always very devotional. Even after the Mass, she would remain kneeling in prayer. That time of devotion and Adelaide's prayerful presence made a deep impression on me, and the Sacred Heart of Jesus became part of my spirituality.

I became my mother's companion and support. I was very deferential toward her and would do whatever she asked. She was a great homemaker and would begin to clean as soon as everyone left for school. I would help her with housework; I liked helping her make the beds. I remember her saying, "Jimmy, you are the only one that will do what I ask when I ask it."

When shopping, she would take me with her. We would get dressed up and head downtown on the streetcar. She would drag me, sometimes literally, through Horne's Department Store across the slick floors. The reward for my not-so-good participation was a stop at Reamers in downtown Pittsburgh for a hot fudge sundae; that was the best thing ever!

Sometime after Joan died, we moved from a duplex to a house at 3103 Ashlyn Street. I think that was part of my dad's effort to change the dynamic of our family life. Dad rented a house with a nice front porch and backyard.

Early Family Life and Community

We are shaped by where we grow up and the people around us. There was a lot of interaction with the neighborhood kids. I think about the house I grew up in and the role it played in my life. My parents seemingly didn't worry about me. As I got older, I could wander the wider neighborhood freely, but home was my landing place. I would venture out and wind up at my Aunt Adelaide and Mary's home. I can still draw my childhood house and place all the furniture and items perfectly. Events that would happen in and around that house remain in my memory perfectly.

As an infant, sometimes at night I would wake up crying and go into screaming fits; my dad moved my crib from the little room where I was sleeping to my parents' room. When I cried, my dad would awaken and pick me up. I remember clearly one night he got a badge out of his dresser drawer and pinned it on my Dr. Denton's pajamas. It was from when he served as a volunteer policeman during a flood in Pittsburgh in the early 1930s. Wearing his badge gave me a feeling of security.

As a child, my parents would say this prayer with me at night:

"Angel of God, my guardian dear, to whom God's love commits me here. Ever this night be at my side, to light, to guard, to rule and guide." Angels are given to us as our protection and guide; messengers of God meant to accompany us.

Like every child, I was afraid of the dark and always wanted to sleep with someone. When I got old enough, I slept with my brother Leo. At night, he provided real security and would pick me up from the floor when I rolled out of bed. He was a good older brother, always very nice to me, and would often play and wrestle with me. I would sometimes sit and ride on the handlebars of his Schwinn bike. When I was little, I couldn't pronounce Leo, so I called him Oy. As I got older, he said, "Jimmy, my name is not Oy; it's Leo!"

One of my earliest memories is sitting on the couch with my mother. Everyone would get up to go to school in the morning. I remember I would ask her many times during the day, "When are they coming home?" It would always seem interminable. I must have depended upon them a lot: my sister Mary Louise, my brother Leo (but we called him Lee), and sister Jeanne when I could get her to respond. On my fourth birthday, they woke me up wishing me a happy birthday. I remember seeing a package on top of the upright piano. So I got up on the bench, then the keys, and then the stand to get the package down. It was my first pair of long pants!

I remember as a little guy, when Mary Louise came home from school, my mother would ask her to take me out for a sled ride if there was snow. They would get me all bundled up in a snowsuit. I guess the lines of the snowsuit looked like the lines of a snake. Mary Louise would object to having to take me out as she had just gotten home from school. So one time she said, "Come on, Snake," which became a joke in the family.

There was a lot of fun, joy, and teasing in the house. Lee was 7 ½ years older than me, and Mary Louise was 9 years older. Lee would tease Jeanne a lot, but she was the last one who should have been teased; she had such a poor sense of her own self-worth. She lived, and Joan died—I believe she suffered from survivor's guilt. She was very sensitive and unsure of herself so she would cry when teased.

We would all dance and play games at home. Dad started playing cards with my mother. That was his way of engaging her when she was sad. They were very competitive with one another, and they both hated to lose. At least once a month they would have another couple over to play bridge; during the day, my mother would also have friends over to play. As a preschooler, I would listen and watch while eating candy mints from the dish she always had out. I always liked to listen in on adult conversations.

My dad worked for a bank that failed during the Great Depression. My brother Lee was happy because the school gave out free milk to kids whose parents were unemployed. "Oh boy, I can get free milk now," he exclaimed, seeing the bright side of my dad's loss. After the bank's failure, my dad went out and bought a new suit, top hat, and a pair of shoes. He walked into Union National Bank and said to the President, "If you give me an office and a phone, I will bring in a million dollars of business a year." And he did just that for nearly 50 years. He was not paid by commission but only a salary; eventually, he became a Vice-President and was responsible for publicity for the bank. He worked hard; he was a sales guy. He didn't make a lot of money, but he got great benefits, a large expense account, membership to the country club, and would get a new car every year. My mother would go on trips with him when he traveled to places like Atlantic City. My dad was known and liked around Pittsburgh. He managed the larger clients, mostly businesses and other banks. He did a lot of banking and legal work for Carl Carthauser, a wealthy businessman. Dad had met him through the bank, and they were friends. He wanted dad to be his financial advisor, but dad just did the work as needed. Dad would never accept any money from him, so eventually, he bought my mom and dad a standing television.

Eventually, he ran the bank's annual golf party for their customers, most of whom he had brought in. He wasn't one to give public speeches but was a great conversationalist. He had a million stories and a lot of jokes, many of which were off-color and he would never tell in front of my mother or the children. He also always had funny quips: "Snow, snow, beautiful snow, step on a hunk and away you go."

At the age of five, I was very talkative and would ask a lot of questions. I remember badgering my mother while she was on the phone with her sisters. She was a good mom and patient with me. But by age five and a half, my mom was ready for me to go to Holy Innocents, the parish school. But Fr. O'Shea said I was too young, so instead, I went to Harwood, the public school. Fr. O'Shea lived at the corner of Landis and Sherwood Boulevard and would watch me walk by on my way to school. I liked going to school and especially enjoyed doing art. My family was not good at crafts, but I really enjoyed making things. I came home one day to tell them about a ceramic bowl I had made, and they told me that Fr. O'Shea called and said they were going to let me start school at Holy Innocents; he didn't want me going to a "Protestant" school. I was so sad because I never got to shellac my bowl.

Fr. O'Shea was very nice. Fr. Wehrle and Fr. Kiefer were the two assistant priests and were also very friendly and fun. My dad had bought a recording machine; they would all come over to listen, ham it up, and record records. The family also made records; it was great home entertainment as everyone took turns to tell jokes or sing a song.

I remember the first day my mother walked me to school at Holy Innocence. There was a low wall around the property of the church that was very inviting to climb up on. I would walk across the street, catty-corner, and then up the street a little farther was a flight of stairs, and up the stairs was the playground of the school.

Mothers often cried when their children started school. I was the last of mom's children to begin school, and she too cried, even though she was ready for me to have something to occupy my time and amusement. While she enjoyed my presence, she was ready for me to be out of the house and have a new outlet for my questions. I was nervous starting after the school year had already been in session for a week, but the sisters made me feel welcome…

Holy Innocents and The Influence of Believers

My years at Holy Innocents are so clear in my memory. The Sisters of Charity was a religious order that staffed the school. The foundress of the order, Elizabeth Ann Seton, was a widowed mother of several children who died due to illness while in her arms. She is the only American-born canonized saint. Canonized by Pope John Paul II, Elizabeth founded the first Catholic girls' school in America and also the first American order of the Sisters of Charity. She had a real appreciation for children, and the nuns all seemed to carry her spirit into the classroom. They were really friendly and kind. A couple stand out in my memory. However, in 2nd grade, I had a teacher—I think her name was Sister Orange (or something like that)—who was very business-like. She wasn't really cozy or warm like the others.

I was born left-handed, but when I started at Holy Innocents, the nuns insisted that I write with my right hand. If I started using my left hand, they would take the pencil out of my hand and move it to my right hand. Around that time, I also started to stammer. It was especially pronounced on hard consonants (like B's and R's). It made me afraid to ask or answer questions in class, as I wasn't always able to speak smoothly. Generally, my teachers would help me find the word or the correct pronunciation but I was always worried that I wouldn't be able to get my words out.

In the 3rd and 4th grades (the classes were combined), Sister Jane Francis was my teacher. She was very small in stature, and when she stood beside my desk while I was seated, I was almost as tall as she.

What my friend Jim and I remember, even later as adults, is that Sister Jane Francis was very interested in politics and was a democrat. We used to plan to ask her a political question to get her off track from the lesson, as she was led into discussing party politics.

I sat next to a girl named Lita Dallas. She had a scented hanky with potpourri in it. I didn't like the aroma, so I didn't like to sit next to her, even though I liked her. I remember we sat in circles and learned to read.

I can still picture my neighborhood and my friends. There was a girl up the street named Gretchen who became a friend. A few houses beyond hers lived Bobby Wheeler. We were good friends for years. He had an older sister, Sissy Wheeler, whom I thought of as a girl-friend. His mother was really nice to me. I remember asking her one day if I could sit on a cloud, and she explained why that wasn't possible. The Berg family, who owned the pharmacy, had several boys. Jim Kavalick was kind of tough; he was their friend and would fight battles on their behalf.

When I was 11, I was in a Boy Scout parade, and we passed a boy who was making fun of the Boy Scouts. I got out of line and said to him that he shouldn't be doing that. He asked if I wanted to make something of it, and I said yes. So we arranged to meet behind the high school. I could never punch anyone in the face; I didn't like that. He was probably about my age. I was good at wrestling, so I wrestled him to the ground and won. I was proud of that and how I defended the honor of the Boy Scouts.

Jimmy Myers became my school friend in first grade. He was older than me by nine months, so he was already six when we met. He lived on the opposite end of Ashlyn Street, where I grew up. That's where our primary doctor also lived. I would mostly see Jim at school, and then later, as we grew older, we would play sports together after school.

We would go up to a neighbor's house to play basketball. We played football and baseball together in 7th and 8th grade. My brother Lee coached the football team. He was really a good coach and had played in both high school and college. I remember getting up on a Saturday morning and putting on a ton of socks to stay warm and fit into the shoes I had. I wasn't very big, but I was determined and played very hard.

In baseball, I was not very good. But I tried my best and was usually put on 2nd base—not the most honored position. I was always small, all the way through high school. I wasn't self-conscious; I just tried harder. Jim was a good natural athlete. We played baseball in a park behind our house; we walked down the tar road, turned into the pool area, and then continued to the picnic area and baseball field.

I remember one afternoon in seventh grade, I fell into a stone ditch while playing and was knocked out. Jim ran to the house to bring back my sister Mary Louise. She picked me up and carried me up the hill. She got some hydrogen peroxide and cleaned up my cuts. I felt very secure with her, and she was always very nice to me. I would sit at her vanity and watch her get ready. One time, I accidentally dropped and broke a bottle of her expensive perfume, and that was like the crime of the century. Needless to say, she was very upset.

Father O'Shea's niece, Mary Neff, lived across the street in a big, beautiful home. Her son Billy, in addition to Jim Myers, was my earliest friend. He was troubled but kind, and we had a lot of adventures together. Somewhere along the line, when we were out of our teenage years, Billy took his life. That must have been a terrible blow to his family. I was away studying with the Marianists and wasn't able to attend his funeral.

There was another kid, Bobby Boehm, who was from Oklahoma and spoke with an accent. He was a nice kid and became a good friend of Jim Myers and me. He and I were the smallest kids in the class in elementary school.

When it came time for our Holy Communion in 2nd grade, I was so small that I wanted to reap the benefit and be first in line, but Bobby was even smaller, so he was first. Every year, the church had devotion to the Eucharist, the feast of Corpus Christi. In preparation for the communion, we had to take classes and practice walking in; there was a strict nun with a ruler who would crack knuckles for misbehavior. I guess somebody had to keep order.

For my First Communion, I had to wear a pantywaist (an inside shirt with buttons that attached to your pants on the inside and held up your socks). I was so embarrassed by that pantywaist; I was old enough to know boys don't wear those. I wore all white with a new pair of shoes. My aunts Adelaide and Mary provided most of my new clothes.

Dressed for my first communion at Aunt Mary & Adelaide's house

When I got to 4th grade, Gerry Henry, my cousin, moved to our neighborhood and started to go to school with us. My aunt was always telling my Uncle Jim, who worked for American Standard Plumbing, to get a job in Pittsburgh. Eventually, he and they did move. Gerry was like a little Shirley Temple. She was a year and a month older than me. She had curly hair and was quite pretty. She would come over, and we would play in the backyard. I was very good in school. Jim and Gerry were both good students and good competition. Gerry and I were the finalists in the spelling bee. Jim and I finished among the top of our class.

On the way to and from school, we were encouraged to stop and make a visit at the church. When I would walk by on my way to Billy Neff's, I would stop into the church to make a prayer at the altar.

I always liked going to church. I liked Father Wherle's sermons; he always preached about Jesus. Christ was the center of every sermon. It made a real impression on me. I never argued with going, or later on, serving as an acolyte. December 10, 1943, was my first day to serve as an acolyte; I was in 5th grade. I know the exact date because my dad wrote it on the cassock, along with my name and phone number. I had to learn the Latin responses before I could serve. I would practice after school, both the serving and the recitation of the Latin responses. I continued to serve for years. Because I lived close to the school, they would often call and ask me to serve at funerals or weddings, even interrupting school classes.

Early on, I was recruited to sing in the church choir. There were several feast days that I really enjoyed, including Christmas and Easter. Another was the feast of Corpus Christi, a devotion to Jesus and the Eucharist, which happened in June. It was beautiful. The adults would come too. I was in the choir for Holy Innocents; we would sing all the songs in devotion to Jesus and the Eucharist, and the whole congregation would parade around the church and sing. I loved the music and the hymns.

In May, we had another celebration; we would go and pick flowers from the neighbors' yards and bring them to the altar. Throughout May, we had a devotion every day at the start of school and sang "Bring Flowers of the Rarest."

I was immersed in the faith and church as a young child, and all of these experiences and the enjoyment I felt in each of them made an impression and took hold in my spirit. I wasn't necessarily cognizant of what was happening, but I believe the nuns were seeing this development in me.

Sister Teresa Mary was my 7th-grade teacher. My heart would go out to her because she was so kind and full of love and faith. The kids would give her such a hard time, and one day she broke out in tears. It had a huge effect on me. Here was someone who really cared, put herself on the line, and was taking it all on from the unkindness of the kids.

I remember leaving school one day in March; I was 13 and let out a yelp at the excitement of springtime. Sister Bernadine was standing at the bottom of the stairs with her family. My yelp embarrassed her, so she sent me upstairs to the schoolroom and came in and paddled me.

In middle school, the nuns would call the house and ask if James would go get ice cream for them. I would go to Berg's Pharmacy ice cream counter, and they would pay me a quarter for my service.

The people in our neighborhood were friendly and helpful. I did odd jobs for different families, such as raking leaves and cleaning out the ashes from the coal furnaces. I liked to make money and be helpful. It was nice to have spending money to go to the movies and to Berg's Pharmacy and Ice Cream store. We were middle class during the Great Depression and always on the verge of going broke. We were never without what we needed, but we were not always able to buy the food we wanted during the Depression; then food became rationed during World War II. My mother would run the bill up sometimes and spend too much at the department store or at the grocery store with Bill Aster. My father would have to go in and negotiate a payment plan. Mom had a lot of people to feed, and there were teenagers. I would get what was left. I was like the puppy they would throw scraps to. I remember having corn flakes and white toast for breakfast with butter and jelly, grilled cheese and soup for lunch; I liked chicken and rice the best. Sometimes, Mom would talk Mr. Aster into sending things we didn't normally have, which was kind of special. I think he was nice to us because we were a family of four children.

The reality of the death of family and friends interrupted moments in my time of growing up. At about age 10, I wandered into the upstairs of my aunts' house. My Great Aunt Ellie was dying; she couldn't catch her breath. Aunt Adelaide and my mom were there, and I was with the family to watch her pass. It was a stark moment. I remember taking that in as a boy, not being shielded from it but absorbing the magnitude of it. In sixth grade, Barbara Anne McGinley died of meningitis very suddenly. In seventh grade, we were playing baseball, and a boy on the team was hit in the temple, which caused bleeding in his brain and resulted in his dying. I remember that so clearly. Prior to that, in eighth grade, Marie Schmidt lost her parents in an auto accident. I remember going to the funeral and awkwardly expressing condolences. We used to go to her house because she had electric toys, including a flying airplane. All the funerals were held at church.

Family History

My maternal grandfather, James John Healy (the Irish pronounced the name like 'Haley'), grew up in Glendalough, Ireland. As a boy, he would hide in the high hedges when the English military came by on horseback; they were called the 'Black and Tans'. There weren't a lot of English, but they made their unfriendly presence known. An English gentry was given the Healy family's farm by the English government that controlled Ireland. After losing his land, the only work my great-grandfather could find was working for the same English gentry who had taken it. My grandfather grew up in all of that; at 18, he immigrated to America in his late teens, setting sail from Cork and arriving at Ellis Island on his own. Seeing the Statue of Liberty was a great thrill for him and a sign of a new life. He lived for a while with a cousin who was a nanny to a wealthy family in Boston. The tradition was that whoever came before would look after the one who just arrived. However, he didn't stay long; he wanted to start his own business and moved to Pittsburgh. He procured a horse and a cart and began to make deliveries from one place to another. James had a great personality and was known as the most gracious guy in town. This helped him gain a lot of business. Somewhere along the line, he met Sadie Kearney, a young second-generation Irish girl. They soon married. They lost three baby girls before my mother was born. They prayed to Saint Elizabeth for intercession, so when my mother was born, they named her Elizabeth. My grandfather was a true Irishman and he drank. Grandma Sadie told him, "James, you'll have to stop, or you'll have to leave." He was a romantic, and my grandmother was a matter-of-fact person. So, he stopped drinking. My grandfather had a very heavy Irish brogue and was a delightful man. Aunt Adelaide used to imitate his accent.

My mother and grandfather (and namesake) James Healy ~1900

One time in downtown Pittsburgh, he was walking down the street when some lye fell from the construction on a roof into his eye; it was terribly painful. He was a man of faith and went to the priest for prayer, and he was healed instantly.

I remember meeting my grandmother Sadie in kindergarten. But I never met my grandfather; he died of a heart attack at the age of 54.

My grandmother had a maiden sister, Ellie; she was taken care of by my grandparents, and my mother grew up with her Aunt Ellie there. Ellie was very religious—to her own detriment, as she would worry greatly about her faults and the state of her soul. She was either scrupulous or an introvert. I remember Ellie visiting when I was a boy. She would always go to the Five & Dime store to get me something. I remember her as being serious but friendly and generous. She was really kind to everyone in the family. She was a tiny woman, with small dimensions. At some point, my brother was in a contest at Burg's Drug Store to win a Schwinn bike. To win, he had to find the woman with the smallest foot in Sheridan. Aunt Ellie won, and he won the bike.

My mother was the oldest of four daughters: Elizabeth, Adelaide, Mary, and Eleanor. My mother was named Elizabeth Anena, and her nickname was Bessie; she was a go-getter and a protector of Adelaide, who was tenderhearted and an easy target for bullying. My mom was slender but tough and would always step into the fray on Adelaide's behalf. They remained very close throughout their entire lives and spoke every day. When my mother was dying, she said, "I'm really looking forward to seeing Addie."

Aunt Adelaide (left), Grandfather James Healy, Grandmother Sadie, Eleanor (baby), Aunt Mary, and my mother (Elizabeth) on the right

Adelaide provided prayerful, emotional, and spiritual stability to the family. She would accompany my mother to the monthly Friday devotion that helped stabilize her emotional turmoil after the death of Joan.

When my grandfather died, Adelaide took over the family business: The J.J. Healy Transfer. The business mostly delivered local goods to stores and pharmacies. Adelaide was smart and could manage the books and solicit and manage business. But she was also easily subject to hurt feelings when dealing with the rough-and-tough drivers.

So, my dad would step into the fray as the tough guy and deal with the truck drivers. I remember going with him as a kid into the office and garage and seeing the spittoon. I was probably four or five. The trucks were older and quite old-fashioned looking. I loved being out with my dad and spending time in the office at the garage. I remember playing on the typewriter.

JJ Healy Transfer truck, my grandfather's business

As a young woman, Adelaide fell in love with Patrick Fitzpatrick, and they wanted to marry. He joined the military and became a sergeant. He taught me how to march. Pat had been married as a very young man, and church law would not let him enter into another marriage without a special dispensation from the Catholic Church. That was a slow and expensive process, so their marriage was continuously delayed. Adelaide had a priest, Father Sebastian, who became her spiritual adviser. She held out for Pat for many years but wouldn't cross the line to marry if he didn't get the dispensation. After so many years, he wrote her a letter telling her that he was coming to Pittsburgh and wanted to get married so she could return with him to the army base, and if she didn't, then he would break it off. Adelaide said with great pain that she would never do that without clearance from the church. Pat finished his furlough and left, never to return.

Adelaide stuck to her decision, and Pat stuck to his guns. Aunt Adelaide holding the line made a real impression on me. I really liked Pat, and he treated me nicely. I felt badly for her that she couldn't reconcile her faith and beliefs with her love for Patrick.

At that time, Adelaide was busy running the family business. Aunt Mary was a model schoolteacher. Students were often brought in to watch her for training. My aunts visited our home often. Aunt Mary was my godmother and was very kind, but I could feel the warmth from Aunt Adelaide every time she hugged me. My dad was a real help to Adelaide in keeping the business going. She never offered him any monetary payment for that, and he would not have accepted it anyway. But she compensated for that in the ways she supported the family. Adelaide and Mary would buy clothes for us kids growing up at the holidays and the start of the school year. When I was older, I learned the Irish folk song "Mary the Rose of Tralee"; I would sing it to Aunt Mary, and she loved it.

Mom, Aunt Mary and Aunt Adelaide

Eleanor was the youngest of the four sisters. As the youngest daughter, she was greatly favored, and she took advantage of it. But I liked her. She married Jim Henry, and they had three daughters and one son: Gerry, Sally (a beautiful girl who became a nurse), James Henry (named after my uncle and godfather James), and the youngest was Eleanor, and they called her Pinkie. They lived in Kansas City, and then Evanston, Illinois, which was a 500-mile drive. I really liked visiting them, and I was close to those cousins. I was excited because they had squirrels – but then I heard they bit! Eleanor always wanted to move back to Pittsburgh and would push Jim to apply for a transfer. He worked for Standard Plumbing in sales in the main office. They finally moved to Mt. Lebanon, and so we would see them more often. In 4th grade, Gerry and I were at Holy Innocents together.

My grandmother Sadie and Aunt Adelaide on a visit to see family in Ireland

My Father's Side of The Family

My grandmother, Molly Donoughue, and my grandfather, William Frederic Short, were teenagers when they met and fell in love. She was a beautiful young woman and strong in spirit. They ran away as teenagers to get married, which was a big scandal in those days. Molly's family, the Donoughues, were Irish and owned a hotel in Johnstown, PA; I can still see the bar in my mind— it was a beautiful piece of wood. She was a loving mother, but because she and my grandfather were both alcoholics, they weren't enough as parents. There were three kids in my dad's family: Julia, my dad Leo Napoleon (named after his father), and the third child was Helen. Julia, as the firstborn, bore a lot of the burden and stress of having alcoholic parents. She didn't grow up in a very secure way and was not able to be sustained in that environment. So, as soon as she could, she got out of town and moved to Washington, DC, where she met a foot doctor. They married and had four children: a twin boy and girl, and two other children who went into the military. Every once in a while, they would come to visit in Pittsburgh, but they didn't have an emotional connection with my grandparents.

Aunt Julia   *Aunt Helen*

Helen was a nice lady. She and her husband moved to Cincinnati, and I used to visit them when I was a Marinanist and had my license. Helen had a youthful spirit and continued to work at a department store in her older years. My Uncle Bill was a traveling salesman. He wasn't reliable by family standards, but they managed to stay together, and they were always very hospitable to me. They had three children. Their oldest child, Jeanmarie, was a strikingly beautiful girl, a cheerleader, and her fiancé was a star football player. He went off to the military, and when he returned, he became very possessive and jealous; he was always threatening her. She really was beautiful and a very kind person. She would continue to call me after I became a priest. Even after Jeanmarie left him and went into hiding, she didn't want to divorce him. She had a boyfriend named Rudy, who was very kind to her, yet she didn't want to divorce and remarry. In her mind, this was worse than living with this guy whom she really loved. Even as a Roman Catholic priest, I could see that her husband was abusive and that Rudy was so good to her. I had encouraged her to divorce him and marry Rudy. I think this really shocked her that I would advise her of this. Like Adelaide, she wasn't willing to cross that line.

My father's paternal grandfather was John Courteau. Courteau was the original family name, a derivative of Cort, which means "short." The family first arrived from France to Vermont and then to Johnstown. Somewhere along the line, they changed the last name to Short to sound more American. John became an engineering consultant for Jones Lachlan, a company that made steel. He was uneducated but was a very smart man and able to figure things out quickly; he worked his way into the role. It was a big deal to work for that company, and production of steel was blazing all the time. They lived in Johnstown during the great flood, and many were killed. But my great-grandfather, with his engineering mind, had the sense that the dam would break and he needed to move the family up the hill, out of the flow of water, and save them. He warned people to do the same, but not many listened to him. He would come to Pittsburgh on business and spoke French, his native language; he came from an area called French Conté. When my dad would visit me at seminary, he would come out with French phrases that he learned as a boy from his grandfather.

My parents met when my dad was working as a teller in a bank. My mother went to work for a business when she finished school and kept the books. She would go to the bank to deposit the profits and her own check. My dad would catch her eye, and his remark was that "he chased my mother until she caught him." Somewhere along the line, he worked up enough nerve to invite her to dinner. When they started dating, he would take her to an expensive restaurant at a hotel and to see shows in downtown Pittsburgh.

My father came to the house to pick her up and walk to the nearest streetcar. When she came home, her Irish father said, "Bessie, I don't want you to marry that little Frenchman." But eventually, my dad won him over; he had that ability.

Family Life

Growing up, our family life provided stability and peace. It was a happy family life, filled with kidding and laughter. For a short time, I developed a fake Spanish accent and would answer my dad in that accent. Eventually, he would say, "Jimmy, stop it."

My parents were very devoted to the family. My dad would go down early in the morning to put fresh coal on the furnace to warm up the house. I remember the truck coming to unload the coal. They would pour it down a chute into the basement window. Mr. Rowan lived across the street. He worked for the mayor, and I remember that he went to church every morning. At the age of 10 or 11, he hired me to empty their bucket of ashes from their furnace; everyone had coal at that time.

We had a nice house with three bedrooms; my sisters shared a room, and once I reached the age of five, I shared a room with Lee. There was a young Black woman who would come to stay and help sometimes. In the mornings, we would have toast with jam and tea with milk (which was delivered on our porch), and then I would go off to school, which was diagonally across the street.

My dad would come home from work, lie down on the couch, and fall asleep. On spring days, I would want him to go out and throw a baseball with me. My mother would have dinner ready at 6:00 p.m. every day, and she always cooked a big Sunday meal, a roast of either lamb, beef, or chicken. One time, we had guests for dinner during the week, and so we had meat. At the table, I exclaimed, "Oh boy, Sunday gravy!" That became a family joke. Everyone had their assigned seat. I would sit next to Lee, and my sisters sat across from us.

My brother Lee was my most influential sibling, the idol that I looked up to. My sister Mary Louise was always very kind to me. She was very pretty and smart. She had skipped a grade, so she always looked young for her grade level. She had a very nice way about her, but she was also a spitfire and a bit spoiled as the first child. She and Lee would tease each other. They would often argue about doing the dishes and whose turn it was. I would volunteer to help dry the dishes, but no one ever wanted me to help because I was so slow.

Burgs was the drug store near our house. We went there for ice cream and could get two scoops for a nickel. I was so disappointed when they changed it to one scoop for a nickel. They also had all kinds of flavors of Coca-Cola. There was a movie theater nearby, and occasionally we went to see movies. I must have been 4 or 5 when I went to see my first Disney film—Snow White and the Seven Dwarfs.

I liked to go swimming, and we would swim a lot in the summer. We went to South Park Pool, where there was a stone tower that I could jump from into the water. At home, we would sing songs and sometimes dance; we would often gather to listen to serial programs on the radio. Jack Benny was a favorite; he was funny! Mary Louise really liked The Shadow; it was very suspenseful and began with the sound of a squeaking door and the words, "The Shadow knows!" She was an avid reader and belonged to the Book of the Month Club.

Every once in a while, my mom would declare, "Today we are going to have a picnic." Adelaide and Mary would come, and we would all go to the park. I loved picnics; the sandwiches always tasted better. Kennywood was an amusement park, and it was a big excitement to go there every year. It was where you learned to be brave, try new experiences, and ride the roller coasters. I was sort of brave, but not really. But I did it.

As we got older, we could go to the movies on a Sunday afternoon by ourselves. On Sunday, December 7, 1941, I went to a movie with Jeanne; when we returned home, my dad informed us that Pearl Harbor had been attacked. We did not know where that was, so he got out an atlas and showed us Pearl Harbor. The next day, President Roosevelt announced the infamous attack by the Japanese. From then on, every announcement about the war was news that I followed. From the age of eight onward, I listened to the news and read the newspaper; I actually learned to read by following the news and accounts in the paper about World War II.

In 6th grade, my mom convinced my dad to take me on a business trip. He would often make day trips to visit wealthy clients. My dad was good at entertaining kids; during the drive, he would have me look for out-of-state license plates. I had been dressed up to go and must have looked pretty good. When we arrived, I stepped right up and shook hands with the guy he was meeting; my dad was proud. That was very important to him; even as a little kid, he would have me practice shaking hands with a firm grip. His client lived in a mansion in Latrobe, and it was fun to sit on his veranda and look out over the countryside.

When my brother was in high school and I was in 6th grade, he was in a school play as the lead. He was going to kiss a girl, and I was very excited to see it! However, I got measles and couldn't go. I was so disappointed; Lee was my idol. I used to go to all his football games.

When Lee turned 16 and was working toward his driver's license, I was 9, and I inherited his Schwinn bicycle. I loved having transportation. I would ride into Sheridan village; one time, I got my wheel caught in the streetcar tracks. It was a struggle to get out, and I thought I was going to fall onto the very large cobblestones. I was so frightened; I prayed and felt sure that I was protected.

After Lee started driving, he crashed the car with two couples in it on prom night. My dad didn't get mad but wanted to be sure everyone was okay. Lee joined the Navy, and in preparation, he went to Bethany College in West Virginia, where he played football. He scored a touchdown against the University of Pittsburgh. I was so excited and told all my friends.

My sister Mary Louise was in secretarial school then. She was a good typist and could take shorthand. She was very bright, but Dad didn't believe they should spend money on her going to college. She had a lot of suitors. Rodge Warneth was a kid she grew up with, but she wasn't really interested in him. Rodge's dad had a real estate office next door to the barbershop where I got my hair cut. Rodge would slip into the barbershop to sit next to me and ask about Mary Louise. He finally got up the nerve to ask her out, and Mom insisted she go. So Mary Louise dressed in a frumpy, all-black outfit to try to discourage him. After high school, Rodge joined the Army Air Corps and became a pilot. It is amazing what the uniform did to help pique Mary Louise's interest in him. They dated and eventually were engaged. During his time in the service, they exchanged letters, and he would send her gifts. Their romance was tragically interrupted when Rodge was killed during a crash while conducting a training exercise in Virginia. I remember the Saturday morning when Fr. Worley, the priest, came to our front door, asked for Mary Louise, and told the whole family that Rodge had been killed. This was devastating for her and the whole family. We knew a few people who died in the war. My father was offered a commission as a Major and had contemplated joining the army early on in the war, but my mother absolutely forbade it.

As time went on, Mary Louise was working as a secretary for Koppers Company, and there were three men who wanted to date her, one of whom was married… When my dad found out, he reacted very strongly. He got the man's number, called him, and said, "I have a gun.

If you continue to pursue my daughter, I will kill you." So that took care of him!

The other two were Bill Reynolds and Larry Aber. The Abers were family friends and Catholic. Larry was an instructor for the Navy Air Corps, very smart, deliberate, handsome, and calm. He was a good match for Mary Louise. Bill Reynolds was also handsome and in the military. Somewhere along the line, she went on a double date with Bill and Victor Mature, an actor, which really impressed her. Both Larry and Bill proposed to Mary Louise. Everyone in the family, except my dad, was pressuring her to marry Larry because he was Catholic and Bill was not; in those days, that was very important. With the family's encouragement, she finally made up her mind to marry Larry. During this time, I used to spy on my siblings and their dates, which greatly upset Mary Louise. I would jump from the banister to the ottoman while she was in the living room with her date. One time, I remember hearing my parents come home, and I hightailed it to bed. I could hear Mary Louise telling my parents that I was such a nuisance; my mom came up and whacked me for making my sister cry.

Dad would give Larry a hard time. When Larry came to ask for permission to marry, channeling an interrogator, dad told Larry, "Okay, Aber, sing." Mary Louise wanted to marry at Holy Innocents and have a sit-down dinner reception at Highland Country Club. It was a very nice club and proved to be quite expensive. The expense of any wedding preparation always mounts, and Mary Louise, as the oldest daughter, was out to have the very best arrangements, which meant expensive. My dad offered to give them money to elope; very annoyed, she said absolutely not but then laughed. It was a beautiful wedding. I remember we left the Country Club, and the whole family went to the airport to send them off. I was in charge of the rice and continued the role of little brother, trying to put rice into Larry's suit pocket. Shortly after Mary Louise and Larry married, Jeanne met and married Paul Dougherty and had a similar wedding. Dad would often quip after the weddings that he wasn't "broke but badly bent." After leaving the military, Larry went to work for Koppers Company and was transferred to Memphis.

We went to Memphis for a visit before I went to the novitiate in New York. It was so hot. Mary Louise and Larry had a two-bedroom house. My dad, Larry, Lee, and I all slept on cots on the floor. It was that summer that Lee met Pat Moylan. Mary Louise worked with Pat and insisted that my brother meet her. Lee and Pat went on a date and immediately fell in love. While we were still in Memphis, we all went out to dinner with Pat, and everyone really liked her. Lee wanted to stay after our family left to secure his relationship with Pat. He told my dad that he knew he was going to marry her.

When Lee went to meet Pat's family, her closest sister was waiting on the front porch to greet him and acted very hillbilly. It was quite the performance. Pat was the oldest of three girls. When Pat was a young girl, her mother died, and then her father died shortly after, they say of a broken heart. Pat's aunt and uncle became guardians of the girls, and Pat grew up taking care of her sisters. She was very kind. She did very well in school and was the captain of the girls' basketball team. Pat had already been engaged to another guy in Pittsburgh but broke that off when she met Lee.

They spoke almost daily but only met twice that year before they got married. When he proposed, he told her family that he would take good care of her and provide for her like her father and mother would want. When Lee and Pat were married in Syracuse, I was at the novitiate in Marcy and didn't get permission to go. I didn't get permission for Jeanne's wedding either.

When Lee was dying, he asked Pat, "Pat, did I love you?" And she answered, "You were always a great provider." She later told him, "I didn't tell you often enough that I loved you."

Lee began to work with Mine Safety Appliances in Pittsburgh, where he would eventually work his way up from salesman to CEO of the company. He traveled with the company extensively internationally. Early on, he was in Colombia when a revolution broke out. He was worried that someone would come to take him away. He kept a water jug by the door to ward off an attack. While he was there, he was contacted by ABC and asked if he would bring video of the revolution home with him to the U.S., which he did.

My Parents' Influence

I was out to please people within the family. My mother was like that. She was very thoughtful and kind; she never spoke ill of people. She was very ecumenical; for being a Roman Catholic, she loved Protestant hymns. In those days, Catholics weren't supposed to attend a Protestant church, but my mother would go for weddings and funerals. She was very social and loved to be with people.

My dad was a go-getter. Reflecting on the jobs that I acquired, I realized I must have had that same kind of go-at-it attitude. This really helped me when I left the Marianists and was looking for work.

My father was very deferent to my mother and always very loving. He was not romantic, but he was good to her. I remember them arguing when I was in high school, and I would get upset. I never liked conflict in the family. I was the peacemaker.

I think music had a lot to do with my growing up. I liked to sing, and the family would sing together; we always sang on trips growing up. We were a friendly family, happy and laughed a lot, and we sat down for dinner as a family every night. I tried to continue these practices with my own children.

Stammering

Stammering was a persistent impediment as I grew up, especially if I was asking or answering a question. I couldn't start words with a "B." Once I got started, I was all right. It was embarrassing, but it wasn't a secret; I stammered all the time. As a freshman in high school, I had to write and give a talk. Both caused me to be very nervous. Dad helped me write the talk, and I memorized it and delivered it without a stumble or flaw. It was that year of high school that North Catholic arranged for me to see a psychologist at Duquesne University. Looking back, she was probably a graduate student. She tried to figure out why I stammered. Her conclusion was that I was left-handed and the nun in first grade insisted I write with my right hand. I was forced to do that all day at school, so it was a protracted disruption to my thinking. She thought that because of the interruption to my thinking, it impacted my motor skills.

Lee was also left-handed, but he refused to switch. They pushed us to write with our right hands for practical reasons: the desks were structured for right-handedness.

When I started teaching, if I began to stammer, I would turn to the board and start to write. Eventually, I just overcame it. It took concentrating on what I was doing and the things I needed to say. Only occasionally I would regress. I could fake it or cover it with a "da da da da da da."

High School and A Calling

When I was in eighth grade, a Maryknoll priest came to talk to the boys at Holy Innocents. At the end of his talk, he asked if anyone wanted him to come and speak to their families. I felt badly for him that no one raised his hand, so I did. I didn't feel 'called' at all. They were missionaries, and that didn't connect with me. Although when I read "When the Sorghum was High," about a missionary in China who was killed by Chinese guerrillas, it greatly impressed me spiritually, but I wasn't personally prompted to go to the Maryknolls. The priest came, and we sat down in the living room with my parents. He was a fine man, but I fumbled for ways to say no.

The nuns at Holy Innocents intercepted me from going to Langley High School, where my siblings had gone. They had observed my devotion to the celebration of the Lord develop throughout my childhood and education. They encouraged my parents to send me to a Catholic school, but we weren't in the neighborhood of a Catholic high school. I was able to go to North Catholic High School because I used my aunts Adelaide and Mary's apartment address on the north side of Pittsburgh. Jim Myers and a few other friends from the south side of the town also used different addresses to be able to attend as well. At the end of my freshman year, the superintendent said we couldn't go back to North Catholic, although the group included a number of exceptional students and athletes. But Jim Myers' dad went to the superintendent and advocated that we be allowed to stay and grow in our faith in that community. They worked it out so we were allowed to continue to attend.

At North Catholic High, we had religious study every day, and the teachers really worked at it. It was a great foundation in theology. The teachers were admirable in the sense that they were intelligent, very relaxed, and engaging with the students. I never minded going to school there for those two years.

In the fall of 9th grade, I joined the football team. We would have regular athletic days, and I was either first or second in the 100-yard dash. The freshman football coach noticed me and my speed and made me a quarterback. I was a little guy and didn't weigh more than 100 pounds; I was only 13 years old. But I was game for whatever I could do. My hand was not big enough to grip the football to be a passing quarterback, so I would call the plays and hand the ball off to the running back. Many times, that was Dan Rooney, son of Art Rooney— the owner of the Steelers. My dad played with Art on the streets of the Northside when he was a boy. (My dad had a scar on his leg from the metal cleats they wore back then when they played.) I really liked Dan, and he was a great athlete. He got injured playing football and was in the hospital at Allegheny General. I went to visit him. We were in the same grade but in different homerooms. Not only did I play offense as quarterback, but I also played a defensive back; in those days, you played both. I made up my mind that I would tackle anyone who came through the line. The kids would bowl me over, but I would hang on and bring them down. It was a big deal to me that I could tackle the big guys. I was determined to do well and was thrilled that my dad would come to the practices and games. Football played a big part in our lives; my dad and my brother both had played.

In the wintertime after Christmas, I was part of the high school minstrel production. Since I was a little guy, they gave me the song "Tonight I Long to Be Returning to Mother's Arms, My Mother's Arms." It was awful, really schmaltzy, but at the time, I didn't think of it that way. In sophomore year, I grew, and my voice changed. So I was given a different role; I wore a tuxedo and bow tie and sang "Walking in a Winter Wonderland." There weren't any high notes, and I was able to sing it well.

9th grade in the high school minstrel

Every March, they would have a retreat and bring in a Marianist priest. The retreats were very Christ-centered and made to order for boys who were becoming young men. In my freshman year, there were follow-up discussions in our homerooms after the retreat. Brother Roggeman was my homeroom and Latin teacher. He was a young, strong-looking brother from Long Island. He would talk about

Jesus and the role of Jesus in the boys' lives. There would be moments of silence and lots of prayer. The school had a lot of spirit. After the retreat and during Easter vacation, Brother Roggeman invited me to the Botanic Gardens. During our conversation, he asked if I had ever considered being a religious brother or a priest. I told him I had.

The following month, I was driving into the city with my parents to mail a box to my brother Lee at Cornell University. Mom would mail his clean laundry, cookies, and candy weekly. I was sitting in the backseat and told them about the conversation with Brother Roggeman, where he asked me if I had ever considered a calling. As my parents listened, I could hear my mother gulp, and my dad was dead silent.

Brother Roggeman wanted to talk with my dad, so he made an appointment to describe the training that I would go through. My dad was totally opposed to the whole idea; he said, "Jim, they've sold you a bill of goods." He gave Brother Roggeman the reasons why I was too young, and he would not consider letting me go to Mount Saint John in Dayton, OH, the preparatory school for seminarians.

So, in 10th grade, I went back to North Catholic. I was growing older and stronger at 14 years old. My mother was supportive of my desire, but Dad continued to resist. During that next year, I would periodically bring up that this was what I really wanted to do, and my dad would oppose any consideration of the idea. I was so persistent, he called me "The Mule." I was very drawn to the idea of dedicating my life to God, like the religious brothers and priests at the high school. I never doubted or wavered in my commitment. Throughout that time, I grew in my devotion to Mary. I would pester my family to pray the rosary in the evenings. I was so persistent that they would give in to kneeling around my parents' bed to pray the rosary. My dad would participate, but it was painful for him to do so; he wasn't very devout.

From the very beginning, my dad was very much opposed to my leaving home at such a young age. The summer before my sophomore year, when I was 14, I began to play golf with my dad at Highland Country Club, and we grew closer; I was pretty good, and he was very proud of me. After we played, we would go to the bar to drink brown cows (root beer and ice cream). When Lee was in town, the three of us would play together. They had a tournament for teenage golfers, and Arnold Palmer was at the 10th hole as a 17-year-old; I watched him play. He was so good.

I continued playing throughout the summer, and during the year, I would go out and play. I also used that opportunity to catch butterflies for homework for my biology course. There was another kid at the club who was really good, and I would play with him. He spurred me on.

Part of Dad not wanting me to go was that I had become his golf partner. He told me I just wasn't going to go. But I didn't give up; the opposition actually spurred me on. This ran counter to my need to please others, but when something was deep inside of me, I didn't give up.

At the end of my sophomore year, as the deadline to apply for Mount St. John Postulate training approached, my mom put the papers on the end table by my dad's chair (no one else sat in his chair). She would remind him that he had to sign the papers. He was always in objection and would stonewall her, upset at the idea that I should go away. He met with a couple of the brothers at North Catholic, and they explained it was a good education and not a final say but rather a test of whether I had a vocation. Dad finally relented and signed the papers, but he remained upset.

They sent a list of items and clothing I would need to go. Aunt Mary and Aunt Adelaide helped purchase my clothing and offered to sew my name into all of the clothes I would be taking. In August, I was getting ready to leave for my junior year at Mount St. John.

My cousin Tommy Nowalk, who was a year ahead of me and a good friend, came to say goodbye, as did Jim Myers, Gerry Henry, and her family. It was a real goodbye, as I would be gone for a year and not coming home for any of the holidays. There would be only a two-week visit at the end of the first year.

At that time, my paternal grandmother, Molly, lived with us. I had a special connection with her, I think because I was the youngest and around a lot when she lived with us. I remember the night before I left for Mount Saint John, standing outside and looking at the sky, praying for her and offering my vocation for her salvation.

Grandma Molly

Her lack of faith really concerned me. I wanted to make sure she was in God's hands. Later, when she was dying, she was mad at the whole family and wouldn't even talk to me. My mother had taken care of her for ten years, providing everything she ever needed. She caused some real strain in the family. She could be very harsh to my mother, and when she was angry with someone, she would really curse at them. I remember standing next to my mother in a protective way when my grandmother was being harsh or cruel to her. It was wearing my mom down, and my dad didn't want to see that happen, so they arranged to have her stay in the elderly care section at a nearby hospital. She took it as a rejection, and they couldn't get her to understand that it was for her good and my mother's good. She was very self-centered. When she was dying, I went as a religious brother to see her, but she refused to engage with me. Today, I think I would be much more skilled at getting her to open up with me. At that time, I didn't yet have that skill, but I did pray with her. Later on, my aunts Adelaide and Mary came to visit her with a priest from St. Bernard's Church.

Mount Saint John

My parents drove me to Dayton, Ohio, and junior year of high school began at Mount Saint John. My arrival brought me into a whole new world of dedication and activity. There were some hard times, but it was a good environment. Mount Saint John had a big property and farm outside of Dayton. We lived in a big building and had chores. It was fall, so we had work on the farm. My nephew Larry called me "Uncle Jim on the Farm." I liked living there and having work to do. My jobs were cleaning the bathrooms and setting up the altar in the sacristy.

There were sonic booms, and we didn't know what they were. We learned that they were coming from Wright Air Force Base, and it was the planes breaking the sound barrier. That was exciting.

Soon after arriving, we had a week-long retreat. As if that wasn't enough, every month we would have a weekend retreat. I read a book called 'This Tremendous Lover'; it portrayed Christ in a way that I could really appreciate. But even more, I started reading the Bible, specifically St. John's Gospel, and it really impressed me.

As a sophomore, I had read a book called 'God Within,' and the realization that God dwells within us was a real life changer. At Mount Saint John, I became centered on an interior life with God. The retreats at Mount Saint John fed the realization of the closeness of God within our soul. Every day we got up at 5:30 a.m. and went to Mass. We were totally immersed in a religious world; there was no break in the flow of grace and influence in those early months.

Mount Saint John was an extension of the University of Dayton for the education of the religious brothers and postulants. It was a high school, and we met in small classrooms; I was in the Humanities and Social Sciences track (there were six of us). I was most drawn to literature and English; I memorized poetry. I also had theology, religious education, and science courses, including chemistry and physics. I was a good student and did fairly well in math. I liked physics but not chemistry.

I also had opportunities for spiritual direction, and I took advantage of meeting with the Spiritual Director. I was trying to get grounded in spirituality in a knowledgeable way as well as in a personal and heartfelt way. He was able to give me real guidance, direction, and points of action.

He was a priest in his early 30s, an athlete who played soccer with us; he had come from Hawaii. He was a really nice guy, and I liked to go to him for conversations.

The priests were young, nice, and athletic and really impressed me. We played seasonal sports every day: football in the fall, basketball in the winter, and baseball or soccer in the spring; in the summer, we swam. It was intense competition, especially during the soccer games. The brothers who were moderating the games would also get involved and engage in the competitive spirit. It was during those sports activities that I hurt my back—the beginning of what would become a lifetime of back problems.

We had a lot of musical training and choir. I also joined the debate group and enjoyed competitions with other high schools in the Dayton area. In my senior year, I was voted class president. In that role, I had to give talks periodically. I would get nervous, and my stammer would come through, but I continued to do it.

At Christmas, the college-age students would come into the dorm and sing to the postulants. They would sing "Joy to the World" first thing in the morning.

My parents would sometimes visit MSJ, and Dad would always say, "Okay, Jim, time to come home." My brother Lee would visit me as well.

Novitiate, Marcy, Ny

The novitiate is the period of training and preparation that one undergoes prior to taking vows in order to discern whether they are called to vowed religious life. After two years at Mount Saint John, I went to the novitiate in Marcy, NY, outside of Utica. It was incredibly cold there during the winter. There was an underground tunnel so we could walk from the dorm to the dining room and avoid the cold. There was a military base in Rome, NY, not far from Marcy. The planes would fly over, and the natural tendency was to look up. But we were practicing modesty of the eyes, where we learned to resist the urge to look to see anything that caught our attention or piqued our curiosity, so we had to work to not look up.

I really entered spiritual life here, and there was very little contact with family. We could write and receive letters only once a month. The first year was real novitiate, with a focus on studying religious life, the rules of the religious order, and the history of Father Chaminade, the founder of the Marianist order. He was never canonized but was beatified in Rome. He lived his life very much at risk during the French Revolution, meeting with young people throughout the city. At one point, the gendarmes came into the home where he was holding a meeting with a large group of young adults. The gendarmes did not recognize him, and later on, someone asked, "Why didn't they see you?" One of the young men said there was a beautiful lady standing in front of him. Fr. Chaminade was exiled to Spain and traveled through the Pyrenees Mountains. He also traveled to the famous holy site, Saint James de Compostela, where the apostles were all summoned after Mary died in order to be present to see Mary miraculously taken up into heaven. They were sent out to different countries, and Saint James traveled to Saragossa. In memory of Mary, the mother of Jesus, there was a statue called Our Lady of the Pillar in Saragossa. Fr. Chaminade prayed in front of that statue for two or three years, and it was there that he was inspired to found the Society of Mary. He was a prolific writer and emphasized that we are all children of Mary, and she would intercede with the Holy Spirit to form us into the likeness of Jesus.

Novitiate was really a great continuation of the spiritual life we started in high school. We had meditation and Eucharist every morning, prayers at noon and 3:00 PM, and spiritual reading, meditation, and the rosary before dinner. We had monthly retreats that were really fun and inspiring. There was a priest who was funny and worldly. He had given a retreat when I was at North Catholic, and he shared about his relationship with God; it really influenced me.

My first two years of college were at Marcy but credited through the University of Dayton. Everyone had choir practice, and the French teacher was the director of the choir. There was also a professional choir director, a layman; he and the religious brother would vie with each other to determine who had the best interpretation of the way a song should be sung. It was funny to all of us to hear them carry on.

It was quite an assembly of talented, smart guys at the novitiate. We came from different Catholic schools, including Mount Saint John. In my first year, there were probably 50 young men. They were a good group, the best of the best, top of their classes. Charlie Cancelieri from Pittsburgh and North Catholic was a second-generation Italian and one of my good friends. There was a guy from Hawaii who was always cold; he made ample use of newspapers to add extra warmth in his bed. Why didn't they give him more blankets!? Fellow novices would tease him about the packages he got from home with chocolate-covered ants and grasshoppers.

We had great meals; a brother named Al Hochendoner was the cook. He was a real character, smart and delightful. He would carry on in the kitchen, and everyone liked to help out. Cooking for him was an event. For example, on St. Patrick's Day, he would color the pancake syrup green; it looked like axle grease. When deer were killed on the highway, the state police would bring them to the novitiate. Brother Hochendoner would dress the deer and prepare a great venison meal. He would also frequently make ice cream and cakes.

It was during this time that I really grew physically. Just like at Mount Saint John, sports were a big part of our community life. In the spring, we would go on hikes. I remember hiking to Colgate University, which was a good distance from Marcy. At Marcy, there was a big hangar to play basketball in. And, of course, there was lots of snow and ice for sledding and ice skating. It was a great life; lots of prayer, pancakes, and play.

We would have regular conferences with the head of the novitiate, the Novice Master, Fr. Martin. We would have an hour-long lesson with him every morning, and he would throw everything into the mix, including poetry as well as scripture. We were always assessing how we were as a person. One time, I said to him that I thought I had an inferiority complex. He said, "Brother, you don't have a complex; you are just inferior." He came off as a stern guy, but years later, when I was traveling for the Marianists as Coordinator for the province, I got to interview him, and he was so respectful of me and my priesthood. He had to be tough on us when we were young.

In the second year, I took college classes in the liberal arts. I studied French and was asked by the senior French professor to teach the first-year students. I wasn't very good; that may have been an affliction on those guys, but you did what you were asked to do. I guess they knew a bit less French than I did!

I didn't have a lot of visitors during those two years, as it was an intentional seclusion. But Larry and Mary Louise came for a visit with Larry Junior, who was a handsome little guy with dark hair. It was a treat to see them. Whenever guests came, Brother Al would prepare a special dinner for family and friends. I remember we had a German shepherd dog in the reception area, and he was intimidating to see. When they came, he barked and really frightened little Larry. My parents came once or twice in my first year and maybe once in the second year.

Years later, when I was working at the University of Dayton, I volunteered to go back to Marcy to help build a chapel during the summer. I had on-the-job training for masonry. It was hot and hard work; it was during that summer that I drank my first beer.

My brother Lee and his wife Pat came for a visit to Mount Saint John

University of Dayton

For the last two years of college, I went to the University of Dayton. I lived at Mount Saint John and took the bus to campus. I took classes in theology, psychology, literature, poetry, chemistry, and an elective class in biology with pre-medical students. I got a C in that class and actually felt pretty good that I had held my own among pre-med students, as I was taking it purely for interest.

My poetry professor was a very refined, educated religious brother, and I really enjoyed his classes. The star basketball player for the University of Dayton, a nice guy named Bill Uhl, sat next to me. He played center and was 7 feet tall, and as captain, he took the team to the finals against UCLA. I stood out a bit in class, even next to him; priests in training wore black suits while the other students wore jackets and ties!

During the second semester of my junior year, I taught 53 4th grade boys at Holy Rosary School in North Dayton. I was teaching all subjects. They were a tough group of boys, and I heard more bad language there than I have before or since. A lot of my work involved discipline. But I would prepare six different subjects every night. I managed the kids alright, but it took such an effort, and I did this for almost an entire semester. I took the teaching and discipline so seriously and tried so hard that I developed a cough and ended up in the hospital. I didn't know what I had, but the medical staff described it as a partial nervous breakdown. I was worn to a frazzle emotionally and physically. I was in the hospital for about 10 days. I returned to Mount Saint John for a short break and then was sent out again to work with a class of middle school boys. I did better with the older kids (plus it was spring, and the better weather helped). I worked with that class for about a month until the end of the school year.

I returned to Mount Saint John for my senior year and continued to take classes at the university. At that time, the basketball team was so good that I wanted to see a game. But we didn't have the freedom to attend games at night. One night, I decided to stay with a few friends to attend a game without prior permission. It was a great game, and we sure enjoyed it. But we were definitely disciplined upon our return.

UD was a very open, liberal school, and in 1955, I went with a few friends to see Martin Luther King Jr. when he gave a talk on campus. The weather was bad that night, and he was late getting to the talk; we all waited a long time for him to arrive. When Dr. King did arrive, he said he had told the driver, "Slow down. I'd rather be known as Martin Luther King late than the late Martin Luther King."

I graduated from college in 1955. My parents and Aunts Adelaide and Mary came to the graduation, and my dad gave me a very nice watch. Unfortunately, the watch kept stopping, but when we took it to the shop, they said it was fine. We eventually figured out that it worked when my father wore it, but there was some current in me that caused the watch to stop.

Me, Mom and Dad on the day of my graduation from University of Dayton

Covington, Ky

After graduation, I was assigned to teach at the all-boys Covington Catholic High School in Kentucky. I learned to drive and got my driver's license while I was there. I also had my first car accident when I skidded on the ice during that first winter. My driving improved, and I became the one to drive all the brothers to school. The teaching staff consisted of a small group of Marianists, six or seven, along with a number of lay teachers. A priest was chaplain. All of us brothers lived in a house that wasn't very nice at all. Before my parents came for a visit, I painted the downstairs living room. When I took my parents through the house, my dad saw that I slept on the top floor and imagined what would happen if there was a fire. He asked one of the brothers, "How will you provide for Jim's safety on the top floor?" My fellow brother said, "Don't worry; we will get him out first." After two years, the diocese bought an apartment house and moved us into much better accommodations.

I started teaching freshmen Latin and religion, as well as the junior American history class. The history course was really challenging; I had to read a great deal to stay ahead of the class. I had a stammer from childhood, and I had really worried about whether I would be able to teach without it being too distracting. One method I would employ was when I started to stammer, I would turn to the board and write down a key word. The boys didn't seem to notice, and eventually it went away.

I also became the school librarian. In the beginning, it was difficult because I was doing things for which I had never been trained, like organizing the library. I finally hired someone to come in and catalog the books. I volunteered to do extras, including starting the school magazine, Contact.

I started a sodality group, which is like a religious brotherhood or association, and picked out leaders from the different classes. They remained the leadership group all through high school. Looking back, I wish I hadn't been so selective. You can't judge a kid by how popular he is or how he excels in school. I wish I had a greater mixture. I think there were kids who wanted to be a part of the group that weren't.

At some point, I began to teach English and really enjoyed it. I developed my own curriculum and had certain veins of literature; I taught classics in Christian literature, and it was almost like another religion class. Most of the books were so interesting that the students didn't realize they were learning theology. Everyone started 9th grade English reading Beowulf; it was torture for the students and for me! I assigned compositions, and after reading them, I realized that the students were sorely lacking in spelling, punctuation, and grammar. So, every morning, we would spend the first 15 or 20 minutes on those basics. I made it fun by splitting the boys into teams according to the sport of the season for drills; the competition kept them engaged, and they didn't even realize how much they were learning. The kids would get so uproariously excited and noisy that one day the principal came to the door and asked, "Can you keep it down in there?" I graded their papers harshly, marking them down for mistakes in punctuation and grammar. They hated it and thought it was too severe, but they learned. There were two levels for English, A and B (advanced and regular). I had many of the same students from freshman to senior year. There was one student I remember, a smart kid, but he just wasn't interested. I told him that he was either going to apply himself or failure would be the story of his future. He went on to college and did well. After college, he wrote to tell me that he really didn't like me, but he was so grateful for my help in getting him back on track. When

I taught religion, I also tried to make it interesting and personal in faith by addressing problems and interests that were real to the students. We discussed heroes of faith, and there was a lot of morality in the discussions. I also tried to tie the lessons to the seasonal highlights (Thanksgiving, Christmas, Easter, etc.).

I had two classes in US History and was able to take the kids to the State Capitol in Lexington. I asked two diocesan priests who also taught at the school to come as chaperones, but they really didn't help with the students, so I ended up managing it all on my own. We had two buses full of kids, and I was always dragging behind because I was gathering the kids. When I got to the rotunda of the Capitol, I was very surprised to see students hanging over the balcony. It was a little wild and disruptive but harmless and not rude. The boys went to the offices to introduce themselves, talk to the staff, and inquire about their work. Surprisingly, I didn't get any complaints. They even knocked on the back door of the Governor's mansion, asked the housekeeper for a basketball, and then proceeded to play in the court-yard behind the mansion. They made themselves at home. We had packed sandwiches, drinks, and cookies, so I eventually corralled them all for lunch on the lawn. We had lots of food, and the kids really enjoyed it and were grateful.

The athletics at Covington Catholic were great, and the basketball team went to the state championship one year. I would get very caught up in the games and always cheered excitedly. I remember a student once saying to me, "Brother Jim, calm down."

We planned dances on a regular basis. There was a girls' school nearby, and they would come to the dances. I asked the parents to chaperone and at one point brought in a professional to teach and lead line dancing. It was truly fun. We also had regular dances with bands as well as a prom for the seniors.

We all went to an amusement park in Cincinnati. There was a man there guessing ages. The kids urged me to step up. He guessed me at 19, and I was actually 24, which shows how young-looking I was then. While the students were respectful, they did think of me as more of a contemporary, and I liked to have fun with them. I remember one morning I walked into school, lightly punched the first kid I saw on the arm, and told him to pass it on. He did. When I got to my classroom, I looked back and saw that they were all punching each other. I quickly realized I shouldn't do that again.

We raised money for a lot of causes, and every year we would take money and goods to Appalachia.

Overall, the kids were good, and I really liked them. Merv Grayson was one of my students, and when he fell sick with scarlet fever, I visited his home to tutor him so he wouldn't fall behind in his studies. Merv went on to college and eventually became president of the local bank. Later, he arranged and helped to pay for my airfare and hotel so I could attend the 50th class reunion, when I got to see all the renovations and additions to the school. They had torn down the original building and built a new school with a Lourdes grotto behind the football field, a new basketball stadium, and very nice labs in the science building. I also found out that the one boy who was the class's proverbial "bad apple" and a thorn in my side was wanted for murder! What saddened me even more was that so many of the students I had in my classes had died, as many as 20 out of 100, and we held a memorial for them in the stadium.

Those years were a lot of fun, as much for me as for the students. It was a great school, and it is now one of the top private high schools in the country. After five years of teaching at Covington Catholic, I left for the seminary.

Photos from a family gathering before I left for seminary:

1. *Family Shot: Me, Mary Louise, Dad, Jeanne, Lee and Mom*

2. *Me with the nieces and nephews*

3. *Lee, Larry Sr., me and Paul Sr.*

4. *Sister Sarah Marie, Aunt Adelaide, me and Aunt Mary*

5. *The Family*

Seminary – Fribourg, Switzerland

When I was departing for seminary, my parents decided to drive to New York to see me off. We stayed in a really nice hotel in the city, and they took me to a fine Italian restaurant. The next morning, I stood on the deck of the ship and waved goodbye to my parents as we pulled out of the port. I met up with the other three seminarians with whom I was traveling. We sailed across the Atlantic on the SS Constitution, a real luxury liner— like a fine hotel on water. We encountered bad weather, and I enjoyed standing on the upper deck watching the ocean water beat against the ship. I met an Italian family along the way who offered to teach me Italian, but I only retained a few phrases. The entire voyage took ten days, stopping first in Milan and then on to Naples. Everyone cautioned us to be careful with our belongings in Naples. At the port in Naples, I saw a man pickpocket someone. After Naples, I traveled to Rome, and we stayed at the Marianist headquarters, the Marianisti Roma. We were treated very well there and joined the community for prayer time, praying the rosary in Italian. We stayed for about a week and visited many sites, including a concert at the Baths of Caracalla, a visit to the Colosseum, and a trip through the Catacombs, where we read the Christians' inscriptions on the walls. It was so moving to be in the seat of Christianity and standing where so many had given their lives for their faith, including Saint Paul and Saint Peter. While on the ship, I met a priest who worked at the Vatican. He asked me to carry a couple of bottles of liquor into the Vatican for him. So, we went to St. Peter's Basilica and attended a Papal Mass with Pope John XXIII, the Pope with a generous and loving heart. The cathedral was so expansive you could drive a Mack truck down the center aisle. We climbed up the cupola above the main altar; on the way up, there was a Coke machine on the landing—an unexpected taste of home in this holy space! We also visited the Sistine Chapel and were in awe of Michelangelo's paintings, especially knowing he had done that work on his back. Viewing La Pietà, his sculptural depiction of the crucified Christ in the lap of his mother Mary, was a spiritual moment for me.

Walking the streets in Rome was entertaining. We also stopped 'occasionally' for gelato as we walked. Traveling in Italy was fun! I found that next to the Irish, the Italians are the friendliest people.

After Rome, we went to Florence, Assisi, and Venice. We traveled by bus and train, and a few times one of us would be late. The guys on board would lower the window and pull the latecomer aboard as the train departed. We were able to see the works of Raphael and all the artists who contributed to the great paintings in Florence. Saint Francis featured greatly in my childhood, and it was incredible to visit Assisi to see the town square where he had disrobed his fancy attire as a sign that he surrendered his dependence upon his father and his wealth. We loved Venice; the square was so large that you could sit at one end listening to a concert and not hear the music playing at the other end. We visited the glass factory where I purchased a wine canister and glasses for my parents with the money they had given me.

When we arrived in Switzerland, we visited Interlaken and saw the Jungfrau, one of the main summits of the Bernese Alps and a very difficult climb. With a telescope, we could see the frozen corpse of a climber who had fallen, hanging on a rope from the side of the mountain; that's an image that really stayed with me. We stayed overnight in Zermatt where we walked the trail part way up the Matterhorn, awed by the majesty of the Matterhorn and the unique shape of the peak. It was late September; definitely cold and our first experience of snow in the Alps. We four seminarians were very compatible on our trip and had a lot of fun, but we were happy to finally reach the seminary in Fribourg where we were truly welcomed with open arms. The senior seminarians treated us first-years as younger brothers.

There were 100 seminarians: 50 Americans, 25 Spanish, and the rest were French, German, Argentinian, African, and Japanese. Everyone spoke perfect English, albeit some with accents, and had attended Catholic schools all their lives. I had wondered how I would react to living with the Japanese after all the accounts of atrocities of war and torture by Japanese soldiers in the South Pacific. But the Japanese seminarians were wonderfully friendly and humble and had attended Marianist schools in Japan from an early age. They manifested such Christ-like love, so much so that I actually gravitated to them.

My four years in seminary were challenging and sometimes very difficult. That first year, I had an attack of appendicitis, allergy attacks, and I broke out in rashes and sneezing. I had traveled with a big steamer trunk in which I continued to keep my clothes. The heat in the seminary was not turned on until the middle of October, so we would bundle up, especially at night. We were quickly introduced to the University of Fribourg, which had 10,000 students, including seminarians from many religious orders worldwide. We walked about a mile to the university every morning and returned in the afternoon.

Classes started in the 3rd week of October and would break for all of Lent and Easter. This was a time that everyone would practice and prepare for ordination. After Easter, we would continue until the 3rd week of July.

As seminarians, we ate well, thanks to the Italian nuns who did all the cooking. One of the seminarians was tasked with arranging seating at the dining tables; there were six to a table. At breakfast, we would sit at the table and watch the residents at the apartment across the street throw their bedding over the banisters. It was more of a curiosity than anything.

We took a full course of theology with Fr. Nicola, an authority on St. John's Gospel and an outstanding professor. Our classes followed the European model; we sat and listened to the lectures each day, not asking questions. There were 30 or 40 students per class, and we were seated at desks in large auditorium-like classrooms. If the professor said something especially funny, in addition to laughing, we students would bang our feet on the inside of the front of the desk; we called it tapage.

I became friends with a seminarian from Poland. Post-war Poland was under Russian control, and the Russian Consulate would call asking for him. We were instructed to say that he wasn't there and tell them he was traveling. He came to visit me while I was in the hospital for appendicitis, and he was so kind and interesting that we became good friends. Later, we learned that he was actually an envoy to Rome for the underground church in Poland and was the secretary to the famous Polish Cardinal Wyszyński.

In addition to the friendship of the other seminarians, Fr. Vincent Vasey, the director of the seminary, became a good friend. He invited me to take long walks with him through the streets and up the hills in Fribourg. I became his sounding board for a lot of his critical opinions of the seminarians. I found myself defending each person, offering a positive remark to counter his negative ones; I carried a burden of knowing what he said about the others. He was an interesting man; he spoke at least eight languages, including Latin, Greek, French, Italian, German, Spanish, and English. A redhead from Philadelphia, Fr. Vasey kidded me a lot, but he was also a tough man. He was a very proficient writer and wrote daily meditations following the scripture of the day, which he shared with me. He was very conservative ecclesiastically and in just about every other way. This was during the time of the Second Vatican Council, and he was not in favor of most of the changes to the liturgy and certainly not in favor of using the vernacular for the celebration of the Eucharist. But he liked me, and I liked him.

Fr. Vasey taught Canon Law in Latin and would gesticulate in the fashion of an orator, and I did well in his class. I sat next to Joe Yamaguchi, who kept falling asleep, so I would poke him to wake him up. And yet he always aced the class. He had borrowed shoes too big for him and he slapped down the hall looking like a platypus. There were four guys from Japan, and they would write notes in Japanese, posting them on the bulletin board. No one, not even, Fr. Vasey knew Japanese. We would often kid that they were planning a revolution.

Later, when I returned from Brussels, I learned that Fr. Vasey had been assigned the Proclimate General, the Marianist representative to the Vatican.

The Seminary Chapel, where we celebrated Eucharist and gradually moved through the different stages of preparation for the priesthood, was a modern church. The altar and the reredos behind it were magnificent. I was part of the choir, and we sat in the stalls alongside the sanctuary. The seminarian behind me was Spanish and sounded like Caruso, a famous singer. He had an incredible and strong voice, and listening to him, I never had to worry about hitting a note! The music was absolutely beautiful, and we had a really talented group of men. At Christmas, I was part of a quartet, and we walked through Fribourg singing carols. One of the seminarians wrote a musical, and I got the part of a teacher. It was a rowdy group of students, and I worked to organize them (like my student teaching days). It was a great production and fun to be a part of. As time went on, I got involved in conversations and counseling of fellow seminarians and thus was often late for evening chapel, but no one seemed to mind. You could come and go as the spirit moved you, or at least as it moved me.

Walking back and forth to class, I would look in the windows of the pastry shops and wish I had money to buy the magnificently decorated and enticing treats. When my parents came for a visit and we finally stopped at a pastry shop, I was very disappointed to discover that they weren't good at all. They weren't the least bit sweet; the icing was simply butter that looked pretty but had absolutely no flavor.

Mom and Dad came to visit me after my second year in seminary. They flew into Geneva and took the train to Fribourg. I went to meet them in Geneva but was late and missed them at the train station. They traveled ahead of me, so I caught the next train, raced to Fribourg, and then missed them again. Swiss trains really did run on time, and that didn't match the rhythm of my life. When I found my parents at the seminary, my dad had some choice expressions for me (I believe it was Jim, where the hell have you been?). But my parents were so happy to finally see me; they forgave me immediately.

Pat and Lee came to visit at different stages of advancement in my ordination. I would also travel with the kids and their au pair, so I got to know all of their kids during their growing up. My brother always wanted to drive into the mountains, and almost always someone, usually Billy, would throw up in the car. Lee would holler back to one of the older boys to give up their t-shirt to clean it up. One of the lodgings for visitors to the seminary was the girls' dorm from the university and was run by a group of nuns. During the off times, they rented out rooms to the families visiting seminarians. Molly, who must have been

5 or 6, stood at the top of the tall, winding staircase and declared, "Look out, I'm going to spit." And she did, from the top floor to the bottom.

Another time, Lee came on his own and went skiing. The slopes were so steep, and he didn't know how to ski, so he prayed Hail Marys the whole way down. We went out to dinner for fondue and walked down a hill that would have been the perfect setting for a Frankenstein movie. My brother was an adventurer, and his visits were always fun.

Although I was very thin during my years in seminary, we were all quite active and healthy. We did a lot of hiking, biking, skiing, and sightseeing. We went for bike rides in summer or hikes in fall and winter, usually in groups of 5 or 6. There was always snow in the Swiss mountains, and it remained cold year-round. Sometimes the snow would come up to our knees, and we were without snowshoes.

We would get up during the night to prepare food for our hikes, each nationality preparing their own food. We always teased the Japanese students that their rice paper was so thin we wondered how it sustained them. We sat on rocks, turned on a burner, and made fondue; we always had good bread from the kitchen. But it was so cold the cheese froze almost immediately, and by the time it reached our mouths, it was more like taffy. We liked to have little sips of anisette liquor to stay warm.

Seminaire Marianist was absolutely wonderful to study in; it had a whole span of windows that covered two floors. I called it the glass house. We could go up to the tower above the second floor and watch the Swiss planes fly over. They would have to get clearance to turn around in France to return and land. From our rooms, you could smell the chocolate factories, which sounds great but really wasn't a good scent. Every adult Swiss male spent some time in the military, so the train station always had soldiers coming and going. There was a movie theater, and we went occasionally; we saw West Side Story there.

The second summer of seminary, I went to Lago Maggiore in Palanza, Italy, with two American friends, Bill Marshall and Francis Chung. Francis was from Hawaii and converted from Buddhism to Catholicism at age 15. We vacationed with Pat, Lee, and the kids. We would walk along with Pat and Lee while they golfed. There were two women who kept pressing behind us, so my brother finally asked them to play through. They were really excellent golfers.

One evening, we all took a boat over to Stresa for dinner and stayed for dancing. Frank, Bill, and I had a great time watching everyone dance. Pat and Lee stayed at a motel, but the three of us were staying at a convent. When we returned late at night from Stresa, the convent gate had already been locked. I was nominated to climb the wall and drop down into the yard. I was nervous enough doing that, but two barking German Shepherds were waiting for me when I landed. Fortunately, I was able to sweet-talk the dogs into submission. Once the guys saw that I made it successfully, they followed me, and all was well.

I enjoyed watching my brother's kids swim in Lago Maggiore; the twins were amazing swimmers. Every day, the nuns cooked lunch, and we could eat for only $1 each. Lee told everyone to just charge a lemonade to his account whenever we needed it. When we checked out, the lemonade bill was more than the room charge! Danny got really ill from some kind of flu, and I ended up returning to Berlin on the train with him and Pat. We took him to the doctor, who gave Danny a shot of antibiotic in the stomach. I had never seen that before, and it was scary to watch, but within a few days, he was all better.

My parents and Aunt Adelaide came at the end of the 4th year of seminary for my ordination. I was ordained on the 30th of March 1963, the eve of my 30th birthday. Lee and Pat also came with their 8 children. I arranged a meal at the hotel for everyone and taught the staff how to make a BLT sandwich. Unfortunately, they put the completed sandwiches in the refrigerator overnight and then served them cold; it was so disappointing.

The day after the ordination, my parents, Aunt Adelaide, Pat, Lee, the kids, and I drove out of Switzerland toward Frankfurt. It was cloudy and snowy. We had to fly from Frankfurt to get to Berlin, where Pat and Lee lived because the East Germans controlled the area in between.

Day of my ordination at the Seminaire Marianist

Cathedral St. Nicolas in Fribourg where I was ordained

Dad; Pat, Mom and Dad on their travels in Europe

Berlin

We arrived at Pat and Lee's house in Berlin with all eight kids intact; it was always an adventure traveling with them! The house was very big, with plenty of room for my week-long visit. Pat and Lee hosted a large reception in honor of my ordination. Lee asked me to sing "Danny Boy"—not your typical ordination song, but he loved it.

My Ordination Celebration; Aunt Adelaide far left, Pat's neighbor, me and Pat

Among the many guests were a few single men who seemed to stand out, and I mentioned this to my brother afterwards. Lee told me the men were "spooks"—CIA spies. Berlin was a hotbed of international intrigue, always immersed in espionage. People would often stop and take pictures of their home. They didn't have Military Police guard the house, but they were aware and careful. Lee sometimes got bad press in the East German papers, and he admonished me to never go into East Berlin for fear they would recognize my name and detain me.

Berlin was divided into French, British, and American sectors. My brother and his family lived on Imdol Strasse in the American sector. The house had a big iron gate in front. It had been the house for the archbishop – the Vatican Ambassador to the German people. Lee's employer, Mine Safety Appliances (MSA), purchased the house from the Catholic Church. It was in the residential area that wasn't bombed during the war because the American military wanted to preserve it for their headquarters, which was a mile from their home. The military base had an American restaurant and an American chapel. I celebrated my first mass as an ordained priest at the main chapel on the base.

Lee was the Director for Auer, the German Headquarters for Mine Safety Appliances (MSA). MSA provided a lot of equipment for mines in Germany and throughout Europe. They had thousands of products. I went with Lee to the factory and saw a demonstration of a spray used on a mine wall to keep it from collapsing.

Pat, Lee and the kids when they were moving to Berlin

The company was located very near the Berlin Wall. Lee and Pat had come to Berlin in October of 1959, just a year and a half before the Wall went up. When it was put up, it was a big event; some people were caught unaware and on the wrong side of the wall with no way to return. We didn't know if there was going to be a war. Everyone was on edge. The war never began, but there was a lot of intrigue and a lot of spying; many people were killed trying to scale the wall.

While I was in Berlin, Fr. Darby, the Provincial Superior of the Marianists in the central US, came for a visit. In hindsight, I think he was there to assess me and determine my next post. Lee and Pat hosted and wined and dined him. I believe they gave such a look of stability that he must have thought I was okay too. We had great conversations during his visit. During that time, I asked for and received permission to attend the yearlong program at Lumen Vitae in Brussels.

After my visit, I returned to the seminary to finish the school year. That spring, I celebrated the Eucharist at the convent for the nuns. I went to give last rites and anoint a nun who was dying. She was having trouble breathing, and while she was taking her last breaths but had not yet expired, another nun took a cloth and wrapped it around her chin to the top of her head in order to close her mouth and help her die peacefully without struggling to breathe. Another seminarian was with me, and we were both taken aback by the fact that the nun had prevented her from taking any last breaths.

While I was at the seminary, I was asked by the Army Chaplain in Berlin (I believe with Lee's help) if I could serve as chaplain while he went on sabbatical. So, in July, I returned to Berlin and served as the chaplain that summer. I spent a lot of time talking to the servicemen as a priest and counselor. I went to three different chapels around the American sector throughout the week and on Sundays to the main chapel to celebrate Mass. The chapel was on Clay Alley and backed up to the forest. Clay had been an American general during WW II.

There was an Irish man who hung around the main chapel, and I frequently invited him to visit me at my brother's house. He would ask if he could call his wife in Peru using a calling card. My brother Lee never trusted him, and in time we found out that he was, in fact, a spy. I was angry when I realized I had been duped.

Earlier in the summer, I had met MP Major Paenessa. He was a big, strong man and very kind and helpful. He was assigned to go to the Berlin Wall every morning to meet an East German counterpart. When he went at Easter time, the German major asked him what everyone was doing out that day. He said, "You don't know?! This is the day for celebrating that Jesus rose from the dead." I was impressed by his spontaneous witness when he shared that story.

When I began to suspect that the Irishman was at least a double agent, I reached out to Major Paenessa. I arranged a rendezvous with the Irishman at a predetermined time and place planned by the major where he could detain him, but the Irishman never showed up. Later, I saw him come into the chapel, and I told him the jig was up and I knew he wasn't authentic. He ran out of the back door of the chapel and into the forest. Knowing that he had deceived me, I gave in to my anger and chased him into the woods. I didn't catch him, which was probably a good thing. You could say I was a little naïve. [Years later, I picked my daughter up from the airport, and when we returned to our home in Denver, we came upon a guy stealing food and other items out of our garage. I was so angry that he had done that; I proceeded to run after him and chase him for several blocks. Later, when the police arrived, the officer told me, "You should never chase after someone: you don't know what kind of weapon they may have!"]

I celebrated Masses throughout the week that summer. I had a German civilian driver, employed by the military, to drive me around. Each morning when I got into the car, the driver would utter, "S*** on Hitler." Lee noted that he never met anyone in all those years who had supported Hitler. When I walked to Mass, my seven-year-old nephew Jimmy, who was small for his age, would often accompany me. It was a mile each way, and eventually he tired, so I sat him on my shoulders and used the time to instruct and prepare him for his first communion. As a little guy, he was serious, not very chatty, so I did most of the talking. He was my pal that summer, and to this day, he is my special friend. He is also my namesake, James Healy Short II.

Back at the house after Mass, the other kids were usually there since it was summer. Molly, who was five, typically chased Billy, a two-year-old, around the house; one time she even had a kitchen knife! I intercepted that. Molly was often excitable, so one afternoon, we were sitting on the couch as the sun was coming through the window. I turned on some classical music and stroked her head to try to soothe her. She was completely relaxed, and that was a time that she and I really bonded.

When Lee and Pat announced they were going to have another baby, Packy, the second-oldest son and around 11 at the time, replied, "Ah, Mom and Dad, don't have another kid. I already don't have enough room to put my feet under the table."

Pat asked me years later if the time I spent with them and their family prepared me for marriage and my own family. I am certain that is so. They were a big influence on me. I was absorbing family life again; it was fun and challenging at the same time. I think my time in Berlin, more than anything, prepared me subconsciously for my later decision to be married and have a family. It didn't strike me directly then, but I feel it was embedded in me.

My brother and Pat were very well known in social life, even hosting the Pittsburgh Symphony in Berlin.

It was a fun summer. On Sunday, we often went to the restaurant on base for breakfast, which was always delicious. We played golf at the country club on the course that Hitler built. It was not a course for chasing a stray ball. If you hit the ball off the course far enough, it would go into East Berlin! Berlin was a huge city and was bordered by the Grunewald Forest, a vast forest that bordered two-thirds of the city. It had a lake, but that summer it was too cold to swim in. During that time, the US Military used the forest to practice military maneuvers. Nevertheless, it was a great place to go hiking.

I started learning German with a woman who taught at the Freie University in Berlin. I learned some, but I didn't stick with it. However, I did memorize Little Red Riding Hood, and I recited it to the children. Pat was better at German than Lee; she would do the shopping and would have to speak with the shopkeepers. She also needed to speak German with the nanny, the housekeeper, and the driver. Ana Great was their German nanny that summer. Ana had a tough family history; so many of her family members had committed suicide during the war. She was a sweet girl but had a lot to deal with.

Lee had a big job, and his mind was often on his work. Ms. Zu, Lee's secretary, was German and spoke perfect English. Lee relied on her a lot; she helped him write his speeches and practice them. One time he was giving a talk, and an employee snickered at his pronunciation; Lee stopped the talk and reprimanded the guy for laughing. Maybe someone else would have let that go, but Lee had such a hard time speaking German that when the employee laughed, it embarrassed him, and he wasn't going to let that slide.

Ms. Zu was such a kind lady. She gave the kids birthday presents and gifts at Christmas and made it a point to be an assistant to the whole family. Lee had two employees who would always complain about each other. One day he called them into his office and told them they were going to switch jobs. He figured if they both thought they knew more about the other guy's job, then let them have it. That seemed to do the trick; they both went away with a new role and were satisfied.

One day, Pat took me on a trip to visit Our Lady Queen of Martyrs, a church built to honor the suffering of the German people during the war. The church was built on the grounds of a Carmelite convent of nuns. The nuns there never left the convent once they took their vows and dedicated themselves to praying for peace and reparation for the crimes of the war.

Circling the courtyard were the stations of the cross, and they all were very graphic in their depiction of the suffering of Christ. The actual sanctuary was on the second floor, away from the convent. Entering the chapel, there was a huge mosaic; one edge was dark with dark colors, but as you moved across, the colors lightened up. In the middle of the mosaic was a little lamb that had been stabbed but remained standing. It continued into a burst of resurrection colors. It was truly magnificent. There was also an unattractive statue of the Madonna. She looked like an older, matronly woman holding the Christ child. It was a stark contrast in its plainness to the majesty of the mosaic.

Afterward, we went to a building that had been a meatpacking plant and was the site of the execution of the men who were part of the unsuccessful July 20, 1944, plot to kill Hitler. They were hanged from the meat hooks when they were caught. Those men were all professional people: priests, lawyers, doctors, and military officers. They believed they had blood on their hands for the atrocities being committed under Hitler and felt compelled to act. This outing really impacted me. Pat had gone there previously to see all of it and wanted to share the experience with me.

When October arrived, I left Berlin to start my program in Brussels for a year. Berlin was beautiful; Brussels was a different kind of city.

Brussels, Belgium - Year After Seminary

I traveled to Brussels, Belgium, to attend the Lumen Vitae School (Light of Life) for my certificate (the equivalent of a Master's Degree). This experience was the icing on the cake. In seminary, I had gone through four years of theology and scripture classes taught in Latin. The focus at Lumen Vitae was on communication of the faith; it hosted an incredible range of speakers who were enlightened and active figures in their communities. During the professors' lectures, we were all crowded into a large meeting room of around 100 students. It was a marvelous concept of simultaneous translation in multiple languages. Lumen Vitae was very enlightening and exciting spiritually. I read a lot of books, did a lot of studying, and listened to incredible speakers, acquiring great materials and handouts from them. Over the course of that year, there were 52 lecturers who came from all around the world, including missionaries, those involved in inner-city work, professors, etc. They lectured anywhere from two days to two weeks. These talks really inspired me and resonated because they talked about faith as a relationship with God and one another.

The speakers, in their manner and teachings, manifested the love and power of God. They shared stories and insights from their experiences and studies. For example, we examined whether it was better for a child to grow up in love in a family or with a lot of classic religion. Religious psychologists found that the children raised in a loving family were the ones better able to embrace God and their faith. I loved this concept; it was so simple. Growing up in the Catholic Church, there was a lot of drilling in religion. But with the teachers and priests at Holy Innocents, and with my family, I experienced the love of God which influenced my own relationship with Him.

I lived in a pension near a roundabout. I was out one night mailing a letter at the roundabout when I heard a car come barreling down the street into the circle. The door on the passenger side flew open, and a woman came flying out, landing on her abdomen. I went up to her and put my hand on her back so she wouldn't get up; I didn't know to what extent she might be injured. The car stopped 50 feet ahead, and a man got out and yelled, "That is my wife" in French. He picked the woman up, stood her up, put her back in the car, and took off. It was very unsettling. I went back to the pension and shared what had happened. The proprietors were a middle-aged couple who had lived through the Nazi occupation. The husband was part of the underground resistance when the Germans occupied Belgium. He was a very welcoming man, and his wife was a great cook for the five priests who were living in their home. One was African, two were Canadians, and two Americans (including myself). As a matter of course, we spoke French during the day.

One day, when I returned from classes, they told me President Kennedy had been shot. The entire household was in shock, especially after learning that the President had died. I realized how much people around the world knew about President Kennedy, and we all grieved together.

During the time I lived in Brussels, a call came into Lumen Vitae asking for an American priest to go to a church for the Sunday Mass to celebrate the Eucharist and give the sermon. I readily volunteered; it was great to be back in action. I had participated in celebrating Mass in Berlin, where the congregation was primarily soldiers. After the Mass, I was invited to visit the home of an American family. They had a beautiful home with a veranda. When they went in to prepare the lunch, I saw their family pet, a large German shepherd, chasing a rabbit. A few minutes later, I saw the rabbit chasing the German shepherd. They were friends playing, and it was such a strong sense of innate goodness winning out. It made me think of the lion lying down with the lamb.

During Holy Week, I volunteered to go to a little town in the heart of France. I was instructed to meet the communist mayor at a restaurant. By sitting with him for a glass of wine, it signaled to the town that people could come to the services for Holy Week. I gave my first sermons in French—they were very short and simple. I also had a wedding and a couple of baptisms. The owner of the home I stayed in that week was a little strange; she had small macabre dolls all around the room where I was boarding. The dolls had dark eyes, blank stares, and were spooky looking. To make matters worse, when I first sat down on the bed, a black cat ran out from underneath. It absolutely startled me, and I actually jumped!

There was a couple at the Maundy Thursday service who invited me to drive to their home for dinner. We drove into the mountains to a beautiful village, and I spent the evening with them. They both worked for airlines; the wife, Susan, was a flight attendant for Air France, and the husband, Franc, worked for Trans World Airlines (TWA). We talked about our faith, and he told me that he was at best an agnostic and really didn't believe in a Heaven. I said, "Franc, you obviously love Susan. Wouldn't you like to be with her forever? That's my understanding of heaven. That would be part of the gift of an eternal heaven, to be with the people we love." That really struck him; it was just what he needed to hear. Leaving that evening, they said they wanted to meet me for dinner in Paris when I left the program to travel home. That summer, I did meet them in Paris, and they took me to a fine restaurant that was on the top floor of a high building.

After Holy Week, I returned to Brussels to finish the program at Lumen Vitae. During my time there, Pat and Lee came to visit me and told me Pat was expecting a baby. When he was born, they called me and asked me to name the baby. I chose Michael Timothy (two of my favorite names).

Upon completion of the program, I traveled to Paris and then on to Lourdes, where Mary appeared to Bernadette, declaring, "I am the Immaculate Conception." There had been a great debate in the Roman Catholic Church on how to explain the Immaculate Conception. Because Mary was fully human, she would inherit the natural effects of original sin. But the Church explained that she had been preserved from sin by the Lord. Lourdes was a place of pilgrimage and great anticipation. They had long candlelight processions at night to the grotto where Mary had appeared. They sang hymns along the way. It was a beautiful experience. Most of the visitors were people of great faith and/or very ill. When Mary had appeared to Bernadette, a spring of water appeared. People would visit the spring and get into the pool of water, and many were healed. God uses miracles to get people's attention, but it is the spiritual awareness and growth in faith that He is really after.

That evening, while on the bus to the Inn, I heard a lot of commotion in the back. It sounded like a drunk person. When I got off the bus, I waited for the man to come out. He could barely walk, and he spoke with a slur. He actually wasn't drunk but had Parkinson's disease. I decided to walk with him into the Inn, and I stayed with him and helped him to his room. I learned that he was an auto mechanic from Philadelphia and had an incredible story… his wife had left him, his daughter was in jail, and his son was living on the street and dealing drugs. It struck me when he told me his story that he was not there for his own healing but for his family. I was really impressed with his goodness. We became friends, and I escorted him throughout the town. He had a wheelchair and could only walk using two canes. We went to the baths in Lourdes, where he was lowered from his wheelchair. He wasn't healed, but it was a very spiritual experience being with him.

Ireland

Despite missing my original flight from Lourdes because I was so caught up in the book I was reading, I eventually arrived in Dublin. Upon landing, I took a cab from the airport to the city center. The cab driver was a little drunk, bumping into things and cars along the way. Somehow, I made it safely to the city and then caught a ride to Glendalough.

Being in Ireland was like a homecoming of sorts. I got the story of the family history, met my cousins, and went to the family graveyard. My parents, Pat, and Lee had visited Ireland before me and met our cousin Kate. They had rented a Rolls Royce, and as they arrived, the call went from neighbor to neighbor: "They are here, the rich Americans." For refreshment, Kate gave my dad a water glass full of whiskey; he would kid about that later on.

While there, I went to visit the family of one of Lee and Pat's nannies. It was a rural home, and during the visit, they brought a favorite pet sheep right into the living room.

Cousin Kate was the same age as my mother. She lived in a home built in the early 1700s; a ranch-style home made of stone. Every time Kate left her home, she would bless herself and say, "Let us go out in the Name of the Lord and the Name of the Father and the Son and the Holy Spirit."

We visited Trinity Church, where my great-grandfather put the cross on the steeple. There I saw the family baptismal records, went through the graveyard, and saw James Healy inscribed on a tombstone; he was born in 1782. Many of the relatives buried there carried the names of Healy and Walsh. Many of the family in Kate's generation had left Ireland, including one of the sisters who moved to Canada and my grandfather, who moved to Pittsburgh.

The graveyard was called St. Kevin's Bed. Beyond the graveyard, up on the hill, there were two split-level lakes and a cave that St. Kevin had lived in as a hermit. He had the reputation of being a very holy man. In his time, there was a fortified stone tower that the monks had built in the village of Glendalough that didn't have any windows, and it was only accessible by ladder. St. Kevin and the other monks would go into the tower and pull up the ladder to hide from the Vikings, who came through raiding, killing the priests and monks. St. Kevin was an inspiration to the village, and they named the area after him. It's interesting that the Vikings brutalized and killed the Irish but then married the women. You could say that the Irish women tamed the Vikings.

Kate shared all the family history and took me around the town. She was young when the family had been forced to move from their home on the farm. You could see the farm down the hill from her house. She took me out on the porch, pointed, and said, "That land was ours before the English came and took it away."

My ancestors lived and grew up in that beautiful area sometimes called the Garden of Ireland, and I connected with them in my imagination. As a young boy, my grandfather hid in the hedges as the Black and Tans, the Irish military named for the uniforms they wore, would come by on horseback. The British took our family land and gave it to a retired British military officer. The family was reduced to poverty, and my great-grandfather had to live with the humiliation of having to work on his own farm for survival. During my visit, I walked the road daily to meditate and pray; I felt a deep connection with the antiquity of family.

I was struck by Kate's continued anger at the occupation of the British after all this time. There was a lot of hostility in the older generation, but the younger generation was changing all that. Mareid, Kate's daughter, lived in London and worked for a British movie producer. The British enjoyed visiting Ireland as tourists. I believe the back-and-forth interactions gradually softened the hearts of the Irish people.

Mareid had a little girl out of wedlock, Katie. The family thought it was a well-kept secret, but everyone in town knew. Kate, my cousin, was raising Katie as her own daughter.

After my visit in Ireland, I boarded a ship in Cork and sailed across the Atlantic. [It was a passenger ship but not nearly as nice as the ship from New York to Italy]. As we sailed into the New York harbor, it was such a thrill to see the Statue of Liberty! It really inspired me. I'd been away from the US for five and a half years, and upon my return, I felt like a great patriot. I continued from New York to Pittsburgh and stayed with my family for a while and celebrated another 'first' Mass with my family at St. Bernard parish church in Mt. Lebanon.

Early Marianist Career

Professional photo taken when I started working for the Provincial Superior

Father Darby, the Provincial Superior for the Marianist communities in the US Central States, had stayed at my brother's house in Berlin. He saw me working with military personnel and decided he wanted me to serve at the headquarters in Dayton. So after returning to the US, I was brought on and had three simultaneous jobs: my primary role was Coordinator of Personnel; I was also a recruiter; and I was assigned to the Marianist College at Mount Saint John as chaplain and teacher. My duties as Coordinator of Personnel and recruiter required a good deal of travel. I would come home on the weekend from whatever city I was visiting and then teach at Marianist College for the first couple of days of the week; I mostly taught scripture. I also served as a counselor to the young men living at Mount Saint John. During the second half of the week, I traveled around the Province. There were 500 priests and brothers, and my job was to visit with and interview each of them. We would have dinner, and then from 7:00 PM to midnight, I talked with the priests and brothers.

After some time, the Marianists purchased a home, and I, along with the rest of the provincial staff, moved into High Acres mansion in Oakwood, a suburb outside of Dayton. Fr. Darby had overseen the renovations of the home, and it was beautifully appointed, including plush carpeting; there was even a pool and pool house. Fr. Darby would hit golf balls off the balcony. Some of the brothers objected that it didn't look like living in poverty and were scandalized that it was so expensive. However, it was the Marianist headquarters, and the staff worked diligently coordinating the operations of Provinciliate.

Brother Oscar, the cook, was German Swiss and a real entertainer. He wrote poetry with a lot of wisdom and humor. He had written and published a two-volume book titled "Light Verse for Lovers." He composed the poems in German, French and English. He had a great heart and was a good man; everyone loved him and kidded him. In some ways, he was the house clown, but really more of an entertainer. He was a talented cook and prepared breakfast, lunch, and dinner every day for everyone who lived at the mansion, which included all of the Council members and other staff, including my secretary, Jim Brown, and a retired priest, Fr. Renneker, who had been President of the University of Dayton. Fr. Leon Kretz, in charge of grounds and maintenance, and Brother Oscar also lived in the home. They were called working brothers; they were not teachers or professionals but were very skilled at what they did. When Fr. Chaminade founded the Society of Mary, he included professionals and also brothers skilled in manual labor. The Society of Mary stressed community living, so there was a lot of camaraderie, a lot of kidding, and kind relationships. We were all responsible for cleaning our own rooms and doing other chores around the house. There was a chapel on the top floor where we met every morning for prayer and the Eucharist.

I was on the Marianist Council, and Jim Brown and I shared an office. I had a former Marianist in Dayton help me develop a questionnaire, which I used to interview all the brothers and priests in the Province. I became known to them, and they knew I was on their side. The brothers and priests were very open and personal with me about the difficulties they had. I reported their concerns and views to Fr. Darby, and he was really tough; he would zero in on me like I was the one complaining. I always tried to maintain a positive view.

Over time, I think I earned some respect from him. I assessed the difficulties being experienced to determine if someone needed a reassignment. I was part of a group of five at High Acres in Dayton that made the decision about assignments for the coming year.

We had grueling meetings at High Acres. There were seven of us who met regularly for the Marianist Council, the council members plus my secretary and the secretary to the Provincial. Besides myself, the members included Fr. Darby, who had a doctorate degree in English from Harvard. He was very dominant in his leadership as the head of the council. John Jansen, from Brooklyn, was the head of education in the Province and a smart guy. [It was he who came to North Catholic when I was in high school and got me to go to Duquesne to be evaluated for my stammering.] There was another priest who was responsible for spiritual development and a brother who was the head of finance. He was very business-like and savvy.

The intensity of the council meetings weighed on me and my psyche; I was also listening to and taking to heart all the difficulties of the brothers and priests throughout the province. It began to take a physical toll. As I was driving back from a visitation to one of our religious communities in Cincinnati, I felt a tremendous pain in my chest. I pulled over on the side of the road, where I sat for a while to recover and pray, and then continued home. The next day, I went to the doctor and was diagnosed with an ulcer and a hiatal hernia. I had to get medical attention and was advised to eat ice cream to ease the pain in my chest. Needless to say, I put on weight, and it reinforced my love of ice cream.

As part of my duties, I also interviewed professors and administrators at the University of Dayton. Occasionally, I gave spiritual talks. Once, during our annual summer retreat at the university, I spoke of the presence of God. For me, it was real and personal, and it seemed to be well-received.

As a priest, you never know when you might be needed. For instance, I was visiting Covington, Catholic near the Cincinnati airport, when there was an airplane crash. I was called to the hospital to minister to the pilot and the airline stewardess.

I was traveling so much that it was decided I should get my pilot's license so I could use the provincial plane to travel. During the training, I piloted the plane, and my trainer, who was also a religious brother as well as a pilot, sat in the co-pilot's seat. During one of our flights, we had flown down to Fort Knox in Kentucky when they started shooting tracers up into the sky—we realized we had entered a no-fly zone! I can picture it perfectly in my mind. My trainer told me, "I think we've moved out of bounds here." I quickly changed course.

With everything I was doing, I was only averaging five hours of sleep each night. I had to meet with the brothers and priests in the evenings after they finished their work, typically finishing around midnight and then up at 5:30 a.m. for Mass. I didn't feel like I always had a good presence of mind, so I didn't think I should continue piloting. From then on, I was flown from city to city: Memphis, Kalamazoo,

Cincinnati, Pittsburgh, Covington, New York, and even Montreal, sometimes flying in the provincial plane and sometimes via commercial airlines. It was strenuous work, but incredibly rewarding, and I could really feel the Holy Spirit moving in and among the community of Marianists and lay people.

As time went on, it became clear that I was on track to become a Provincial Superior.

Baptism In The Spirit and Meeting Barbara

It was toward the end of my time at High Acres that I became heavily involved in the charismatic movement. I received an invitation to visit Cleveland, where there were two Marianist high schools and a retreat house, and I flew there to interview the brothers and priests at the schools. St. Joseph's High School was in a nice part of the city and was well-staffed; they must have had 50 brothers and priests teaching there.

Some of the brothers at St. Joseph's had been baptized in the Holy Spirit. I went to their prayer meeting, and they prayed over me in the Holy Spirit. Not much happened to me at that time. When I returned to Dayton, Jim Brown enthusiastically related to me his experience the night before when he had gone to a charismatic prayer meeting; he was baptized in the Holy Spirit and received the gift of praying in tongues. Jim was a very bright young man and became a good friend. He wanted me to go to a meeting at the home of a Pentecostal couple. So the next day, I went with him to the home of an extended family, the Hotts and the Malots. They prayed over me, and I received the gift of tongues.

I soon became a known figure—a Roman Catholic priest who prayed in tongues. I began to attend a lot of prayer meetings. We went to a convent in North Dayton that housed a dozen nuns living in close quarters. They had become at odds and very tense with one another. I went with Jim; we invited them to open their hearts, and they were baptized in the Spirit. They became an extraordinary and peaceful group of believers.

A young Pentecostal pastor in Dayton became my friend. He was a bit rough and tough but married to a peaceful woman. They had a church, and he invited me to attend and sometimes to give talks. I even got my parents to attend with me. Previously, I had felt very anxious prior to giving sermons, but after being baptized in the Spirit, I was freed of that anxiety and spoke with ease. I found that while speaking, my mind operated at three levels: I stayed in prayer to the Holy Spirit; I referred to the notes I had prepared; and I was able to relate to the congregation. Being dialed into the congregation often directed my thoughts and speaking. My first experience of this was during a meeting at the college center at Mount Saint John when I was teaching the college-age scholastic brothers.

Throughout the years to come, I continued to give sermons with a certain ease, led by the Holy Spirit. This was especially true later in my life at Ascension, where I really knew the congregation well.

I went to the University of Dayton regularly to give talks and meet with the young brothers and nuns I was counseling. At one point, Fr. Darby told me not to go to the university anymore. I think he was trying to protect me. He had been going somewhere with a group of young brothers and had provided transportation to a group of young women along the way. At that moment, he had a sense that the young brothers would be attracted to the girls. I think he was concerned about the relationships I was developing with various people. That was the one time that I went against what he explicitly told me to do. I felt strongly that it was more important to continue to support these young nuns and brothers. I felt very badly about my choice to go against his directive. When you take a vow of obedience in a religious order, even when the superior's directive doesn't feel quite right, you shouldn't blindly disregard that order. In hindsight, I should have gone back to him to explain why I thought it was important for me to continue, and I learned from that time that it was more important to be obedient to the Lord through the voice of the superior.

In September of 1966, a Catholic priest was giving a women's retreat at the Dominican Sisters Convent up the street from High Acres. He called and asked if I would come and be an assistant at the retreat. As part of my help, I hosted confession for anyone who wanted that sacrament.

During the evening session, I caught Barbara Gumm's eye across the room, a knowing eye; there was an attraction between us. The evening session ended around 10:30 p.m. and the women retired to their rooms (or home if they lived locally), but Barbara stayed, and we began to talk about spirituality.

It quickly became a spiritual connection. She was surprised that my way of thinking was so similar to hers and that we both had been influenced in the expression of our faith by Billy Graham. I resonated with his way of surrendering to the Lord. She and I shared a belief in the essence of the relationship with Jesus— "I am the way and the truth and the life." We talked late into the night. A nun came in at 1:30 a.m. singing "It's one o'clock in the morning." After that, I went out the front door and back to High Acres.

Over the next few months, Barbara and I kept in touch. Occasionally, she would call and ask to come for a visit to High Acres. We were simply friends, but I do remember she wore a white angora sweater during one of her visits and I noticed how pretty she was.

During that time, I was getting more involved in the charismatic renewal. Barbara also attended some of the charismatic renewal meetings that Brother Jim Brown and I organized, and she was baptized in the Holy Spirit. This deepened the spiritual connection we started to develop at the first retreat. She made a Cursillo in Cincinnati during that year, and during one of her visits to High Acres, she shared about that experience and the priest who had been a big influence on her.

In September of the following year, Paul and Mary Lou Reisinger told me to go visit Bill and Pat Copeland when I traveled to New York for the Marianists. The Copelands had lived in Dayton for Bill's work and had moved to Connecticut.

Bill invited me to a lay-led four-day Cursillo retreat. I went as a priest, but I was there to learn and participate. One of the top executives at IBM got up to give a talk. Five minutes into his talk, the Lord spoke so clearly in my mind and soul. I had a definite impression that God was giving me the freedom to be married and have a family. It came suddenly, like the dawning of a new day, and I knew there was a new dimension I could enter into, one that included marriage and a family and something other than being a Catholic priest.

I had gone down a path toward priesthood as a young teenager. I remember deciding I was giving up relationships with women at a young age and doing it willingly for the Lord. But now other things were awakening in me. I had the sense that there were relationships out there that were waiting for me. I'd been baptized in the Spirit, and I felt a great sense of awakening and life on a physical, spiritual, soulful, and sexual level. God was in the midst of all of this.

On Friday night after the retreat, I celebrated Eucharist at the Copelands' home, and many of their friends came, including men from the Cursillo and their wives. These were smart, attractive, successful young families. I had shared at the retreat that I was feeling called to leave the priesthood and have a family. So this strong group of believers knew the changes that were happening in me, and they were helping me to try to discern what was occurring.

I really felt that the Holy Spirit was moving in my life. The Copelands asked me to go pray for a friend who had been diagnosed with cancer. We prayed together, and he was healed. Another friend of theirs was dying from stomach cancer, so I drove into New York City to meet and pray with him. That night, his body flushed the cancer and illness. I never hesitated to step out in faith, and God was affirming me through His answers to my prayers.

Following the retreat, I was in a very active mode of spiritual encouragement and direction to people. It was a demanding time, but I also felt the presence of the Lord as I interacted with so many people. Paul and Mary Lou Reisinger became an important part of my life. I became a support to Joe Callahan, a former UD football player who was suffering from abdominal cancer. He became a good witness of someone coming to faith in the Lord. He and his wife, Joan, lived just down the street from High Acres, and when he died, I celebrated the Eucharist at his funeral. As time went on, I also counseled Joan's sister, whose husband was an alcoholic. I became friends with all of them and was supportive of Joan's sister when her husband eventually drank himself to death within a year after Joe's death.

Barbara's Family

Barbara's dad, Aaron Gumm, worked at Wright-Patterson Air Force Base, east of Dayton, as an accountant. Wright was an experimental airfield where the government was developing supersonic fighter planes. Living in Dayton, we would sometimes hear a great boom when the planes would break the sound barrier.

Aaron had been the State Auditor in West Virginia. He met his future wife, Barbara's mother, Eleanor, at a boarding house where they both lived. His first wife was an educated woman and a writer; her articles had been published. She had tuberculosis and was in a sanatorium, and he would visit her when possible. In the end, he didn't get to see her before she died.

The boarding house where Aaron lived was home to several young professionals. It had individual rooms with shared baths, a kitchen, and common areas.

Aaron was an attractive young man. Eleanor and a friend would stand outside his room at night and hear him snoring; it was a part of their entertainment (back in the days when there wasn't television).

In Barbara's growing up, her mother, Eleanor, worked for the football coach at the University of Dayton. Aaron would say to her, "Don't encourage Barbara (Bobby) and Nancy (her sister, who is 11 months older) to date Catholic boys from the University of Dayton." Fortunately, when Barbara invited me to their lovely home in Kettering as a friend, a priest from the University of Dayton, we got along very well. I liked her parents, and they liked me.

Stepping Out in The Charismatic Movement

I was on the frontline teaching and preaching, giving talks at Mount Saint John and counseling some of the college-aged brothers, and I was still traveling quite a bit for the Marianists.

During this time, my sister Jeanne was battling alcoholism. Her husband Paul's work had taken them to Massachusetts, where Jeanne had no acquaintances. Away from friends and family in Pittsburgh, she became very lonely and started drinking. Her drinking continued to increase, as did her erratic behavior. In time, they relocated to Dearborn, Michigan for his work. I had an adult Christian conference in the Detroit area and used the opportunity to visit my sister and her family. Paul Jr. was a perceptive and smart teenager. During that one-day visit, I felt the Lord leading me to talk to Paul Jr., so I invited him to take a walk. He confided in me how hurt he was by his mother's drinking and the strife it was causing in the family. This was the beginning of our friendship.

Shortly thereafter, Father Darby asked me to drive to Chicago to meet with his nephew, whom he thought was being called to the priesthood. I invited my nephew Lee Aber to drive with me from Dayton to Chicago and back. Lee was young and faith-filled, and I thought he would be a good influence on Father Darby's nephew. During the drive, we were so engrossed in conversation and my sharing about the charismatic movement that I wasn't paying attention to my speed and was stopped by the police. On the return trip, we went to Pittsburgh to visit my family. While at my parents', I invited them to prayer, and

Lee, along with Aunt Adelaide, was baptized in the Holy Spirit and prayed in tongues. It wasn't long after that trip that Fr. Darby's niece was killed in a car accident coming home from college. It really affected him, and he grieved deeply. I know that I prayed and spoke with him; in those times, I wasn't hesitant to enter into the middle of a situation, believing that God would do something.

In January of 1968, I was assigned to the Pope John XXIII Christian Renewal Center, and I moved from High Acres to Mount Saint John. It was a beautiful center.

In March 1968, I organized a conference at the Marianist College in Mount Saint John. I convinced my mom and even my dad to come. It was an interesting group of people who gathered from different denominations and backgrounds. At one point, we divided into small groups, and I was leading a prayer in tongues when the young fellow next to me said he knew what I was saying. I believe this was the first time I had prayed in tongues publicly and had it interpreted; it was very inspiring.

After the March conference, I convinced the priest in charge of the Christian Renewal Center to sponsor a larger conference in June. In the weeks prior to the June conference, there were race riots in Dayton. We decided we needed to do something to interrupt the riots that were really beginning to take hold. Jim Brown and I, along with a small group of people from the March meeting, went to the chapel and prayed that God would stop the riots. We stood against the riots in Jesus' name. As we prayed, we heard a real noise in the rafters of the ceiling. We had called upon Saint Michael and the angels to stop the riots. We felt the noise we heard was the movement of the angels in God's response to our prayers. After our prayers, it was an absolutely quiet night, and the riots halted.

I wanted to involve religious leaders from around the country to speak at the conference, so we wrote to every Roman Catholic bishop and head of a religious order in the country. We sought a great audience of attendees and speakers. One attendee was from the Diocese of Bishop Fulton Sheen in Buffalo. Bishop Sheen wrote several books, was an outstanding preacher, and had a long-standing weekly primetime national television show.

We also felt it was important to invite notable speakers. Our speakers included a psychologist from the University of Texas and a psychiatrist who had worked in China. We also had a Catholic priest who was a real scholar in the scriptures and had studied the history of the charismatic renewal. Everyone had their own story of how they became involved in the charismatic movement. The psychologist from Texas shared that his wife initially thought it was all made up and unreal. But when she fell and broke her ankle, she was prayed over and was healed. From that moment, she became very charismatic. By having all these professional, educated people speaking, it gave authority and validity to the movement.

So much happened at that conference. I was the emcee and was very nervous.

Some 350 people came to the conference, including a large local network of charismatic Pentecostals. At that time, the Pentecostals were quite set apart from other denominations and vocally opposed to the Roman Catholic Church. To have them attend a charismatic conference at the Catholic Christian Renewal Center and hear speakers from all denominations, including Catholic leaders, really opened the door to the Holy Spirit.

Meanwhile, I received a letter from the Archbishop of Cincinnati, whom I had invited to attend the conference. The letter instructed that the non-Roman Catholics were not to receive communion. That was a real blow to me because I always invited anyone who believed in Jesus as Lord and Savior to receive communion and explained what we believed the Eucharist to be. At the conference, I got up prior to communion, very embarrassed to share the letter, and explained that it was a Catholic discipline. I said we would just wait and see what the Holy Spirit thinks. We had scheduled the conference to finish over the weekend of the Feast of Pentecost. And on that Pentecost Sunday, only the Catholics received communion, but the Spirit of the Lord moved through the whole group, and different gifts of the Spirit were manifest throughout the congregation. It was so notable that God was using that time to reach everyone.

Leroy Jenkins was one of the leaders I had invited to pray over people. Leroy had a powerful story: He had broken his arm in a car accident; the pain was unbearable, and he was so discouraged he decided to take his own life by driving his car into a pole. A woman from the Assembly of God in town had been inspired to go meet with him, and she pulled into his driveway as he was ready to drive off to fulfill his plan. She convinced him to let her pray for him. He was transformed, and his arm was completely healed. But interestingly, he never had fingerprints on that hand after that.

In January, prior to the March conference, I had attended a conference Leroy held at Hara Arena in Dayton, where he prayed over various people. I intentionally sat in the back of the arena. At one point, a little girl who was crippled was led onto the stage. He prayed a simple prayer over her; she was healed instantly and ran down the steps. When I watched him pray over that little girl, the only explanation was the power of God. I went out to meet her afterwards, and her parents told me she was scheduled to go to the hospital for surgery. They said, "Look at her now!" She was running and sliding in the corridor of the arena. I then became a friend of Leroy Jenkins.

On Easter morning following the March conference, I received a call from a nun at the University of Dayton who had heard about me. Her brother John, a high school student, had been beaten up and thrown down a window well the night before. She asked me to visit him in the hospital, where he was unconscious with a skull fracture, and I asked Leroy to join me. When I asked Leroy to pray over John, he invited me to pray instead. It was a big moment for me as I stepped out in my faith to publicly pray for healing. I spoke to him directly: "John, I am here and going to pray for you, and I want you to respond." I continued, "John, in the name of Jesus, lift your arm." He lifted his arm up very slowly; it was like calling down a well into his unconscious state. I took this as an indication that God was healing him. As it happened, I was scheduled to travel to St. Louis the next week. When I returned to Dayton after a week and a half, I immediately went to see him at Kettering Hospital. As I walked down the corridor, I passed a solarium where John was sitting with his family. I asked the family to tell me how he was doing. He was healing well, but he wasn't yet talking. So I prayed over him, "Okay, John, it is time to start to speak again. In the name of Jesus, speak." And he began to speak. That was inspiring for me; I needed to be bold and step out in my faith. All of this occurred in the lead-up to the charismatic conference in June.

My friends, the Copelands, knew Phil Donahue, and they introduced us. I invited Phil to come to the conference; he didn't attend, but his wife, Margaret, did. Jane, a friend of mine who was a nun, and her aunt, who was also in the same religious order, also came. Her aunt had a very serious heart condition. Leroy Jenkins prayed over her during the conference, and her heart condition was completely healed, as confirmed by her cardiologist the following week.

I invited representatives from Newsweek and the National Catholic Reporter to attend the conference as well. We were anticipating a feature article from both of them. But it was June 5, 1968, the day that Bobby Kennedy was assassinated. Naturally, we got very little coverage. Nevertheless, we achieved our goal of bringing the baptism of the Holy Spirit to public notice. People were inspired, changed, and empowered by the Holy Spirit.

Sometime after the June conference, Phil Donahue invited four of us to come on his daily radio program (including Tommy

Tyson and Leroy Jenkins). His show was very popular, and this was a great opportunity for us. When we described the charismatic movement, Phil said, "Sounds to me like a firehouse religion." I said, "Phil, that is just your style; you are a firehouse religion kind of guy." This resonated with his audience, who understood him to be that way.

Around that time, Leroy asked me to be his chaplain and travel with him; that would not have been acceptable to the Marianists, and I declined his offer. Later in life, Leroy ended up in jail for tax evasion, but that became an opportunity for him to minister. He received clearance to travel throughout the prison to minister and witness to the other inmates. On the weekends, he was permitted to visit churches on Sunday. God used the occasion of these visits to convert many people during Leroy's internment in prison.

The Start of A New Calling

Sister Jane, who had attended the conference in June and whose elderly aunt was healed, began to write letters to me. She had spoken at the conference and was a bit of a stand-up comedian. She was a very nice person, had a great sense of humor, and was also a trainer for Montessori teachers. She continued to come to some of the charismatic meetings after the conference.

She invited me to meet her and her parents in Cincinnati during my travels. During my visit, she shared that she had decided to leave the religious order and felt we were a good match. She was so engaging and influential, but I didn't respond at that time. She was persistent in pursuing me, and we did keep in touch.

Earlier that spring at Mount Saint John, when I would celebrate the Eucharist for the brothers, a woman named Sister Rachel would come. She caught my eye; we spoke, and in time we became friends. She was a singer and played guitar. I took her to Pittsburgh; I wanted my parents to hear her sing. She played for my parents and was very pleasant. But my mom was beginning to get suspicious. She could see that I was attracted to this woman with a good spirit. My mom sensed that she was pursuing me.

There was a movie, "Rachel, Rachel," wherein the character Rachel was deeply affected by praying in the spirit, but the whole thing went awry. When Sister Rachel saw the movie, she was so spooked that she turned away from the charismatic movement, and we lost contact after that.

I continued to see Barbara intermittently at prayer meetings and occasionally at High Acres. After the charismatic conference, Barbara came for a visit in her dad's car. I drove around in circles in the parking lot; she was laughing but thought I was a little crazy.

One night during that time, I woke up in the middle of the night and felt the presence of Satan in the room; he walked right across the room, a black shadow, and I screamed. No one seemed to hear me. That was my first awareness of the presence of evil. I didn't think a lot about it afterwards. I think it was a warning the Lord allowed to happen. At that time, I was really stepping out in my faith on the frontline and declaring God's power in the name of Jesus. It was like Satan was putting me on notice. The experience left an impression, but it didn't stop me or discourage me.

Fordham And an Enlightening Pilgrimage

While I already had a very good education, I did not have an American graduate degree. I asked Father Darby if I could go to Fordham to study Christian Education. He agreed I would go that summer after the conference in June.

Prior to going to Fordham, I read the schedule of appointments for the brothers and priests and saw that I was instead assigned to go to Malawi for the following year. I was stunned; Fr. Darby had promised that I would go to Fordham. I stormed into his office and strongly insisted that he had made a promise and I was set to go. So he relented.

By that time, he must have thought I was pretty far afield. I had met so many people, been to so many conferences, back and forth to UD, and so forth. I think he thought I needed to be on a shorter leash. But he committed to keeping his promise.

I sometimes wonder what my life would have been like had I gone to Malawi. I think I would have looked Barbara up whenever I came home on a break. Barbara and I often discuss how our getting together was really meant to be, that it was truly ordained by God. I believe it was God's plan for me and Barbara, and his plans aren't thwarted.

Prior to going to Fordham, I was asked to lead the second year of the Women's Retreat at the Dominican Retreat House in Dayton. I drove to Pittsburgh and picked up my two sisters Mary Louise and Jeanne, my mother Bessie, and my aunts Adelaide and Mary. Barbara came with her mom, sister, and her neighbor, Mary. My family met

Barbara on that retreat; she and Mary Louise developed a quick friendship.

It was on the way back to Pittsburgh that I told my family about my experience at the Cursillo retreat—that I was free to marry, have a family, and be something other than a Roman Catholic priest. It sent shock waves through the car. Their immediate reaction was stunned silence. But they soon kicked off a campaign that continued for the next several months to preserve my vocation. They functioned as devil's advocates, including calls from Aunt Adelaide and letters from Mary Louise, who even wrote to Barbara. She acknowledged the attraction Barbara and I felt for each other but pointed out that both my family and the Marianists were heavily invested in my vocation and it should be preserved.

I went to Chaminade Mineola to live and attend Fordham for graduate school. I had a great Jesuit professor, Father Peter Ellis. He had an openhearted, winning personality, and he became my friend, and I shared with him my lifetime of spiritual experiences.

During this time, I gave a spiritual talk about the importance of God with us, God within us at the annual conference for the Marianist brothers and priests. These were very intelligent men, and they seemed to accept what I was sharing. I was often traveling back to Dayton for work and prayer meetings.

In January of 1969, while I was at Fordham, the Pentecostal Assembly in Dayton invited me and sponsored my travel to a pilgrimage in the Holy Land. Separately, Barbara had been encouraged to join the pilgrimage. When I found out she was also going, I invited her to visit the Copelands with me prior to our departure. The Copelands immediately liked Barbara and knew that she was a real and genuine person. From there we left for the airport and sat together on the flight, as oddly enough we were the only two single people in the group.

Barbara on our pilgrimage in Israel

During the trip, a group of us would go down in the evenings to the Hotel Jerusalem's bar to get a drink. The Baptists wouldn't come, but the Catholics and others joined us. One night Barbara and I took the elevator up together; I was on the 2nd floor and Barbara on the 3rd. On the way, I told Barbara, "I have to tell you something. There is a good chance that I'm leaving the Marianists. And I think I know who I'm going to marry." Barbara said, "Huh. That's like hearing who won the horse race before it's over." I got off the elevator, walked to my room, and pondered what she had just said. Only then did it dawn on me that she wanted to be in the race.

The night before we returned home, Barbara and I sat in a conference room in our hotel in Tel Aviv and talked late into the evening. A hotel employee came to turn the lights off but stopped when he saw us, so as not to disrupt our conversation. In my mind, I recalled the song by the Browns about the old lamplighter. While I sat with

Barbara, my luggage was stolen from the lobby. Before leaving Israel, Barbara wrote me a letter telling me she thought it best we not continue to be in contact, but when I made a decision about whom I was going to marry, to let her know.

We flew from Tel Aviv to Athens. During my layover, I called my brother Lee. He said, "Jim, I just talked with Mom and Dad, and they told me about your decision to leave the Marianists. I want you to get off that flight to Dayton and come to Berlin." So I went to Berlin. For five nights, we sat up late talking as he tried to convince me not to make that move. He argued that I made a commitment to stay with the Marianists, just like he had made a commitment to marry Pat, and my leaving was like a divorce. Remarkably, none of this affected me. Lee was a world-class debater, but nothing moved me from my decision. When I was leaving Berlin, he asked me to call him when I made up my mind. It was such a busy time when I returned that I forgot to call him.

From there, I left and went back to Fordham, where I would often visit the Copelands on the weekends. Leaving the Marianists was the main topic of conversation. However, they were very supportive and did not try to talk me out of leaving the priesthood. They, like my brother's family, were a big influence on my attraction to marriage and family life.

While I was living in Mineola, Dad came for a work trip, and I wanted him to meet Jane. I had wondered if Jane would be the person I would marry. We had dinner together, and he felt there was something about her that did not ring true.

I think what I needed in those days was a strong spiritual director with whom I could talk about everything that was going on in my heart, mind, and soul. There was a priest from Chaminade Mineola whom I would go to for confession and to talk, but I didn't feel he really saw and understood me at my soul level. I don't know that a good spiritual director would have changed my course, but he may have slowed me down. I felt I was really growing, and my whole being was opening up to relationships with people, mostly in friendships but also some attraction.

When I was finishing at Fordham, Jane wanted me to come and live with her in NJ, but I refused. Even though I felt bad, and would walk the floors at night heartbroken by the separation, I knew it was for the best. Instead, I went to live with the Copelands in Connecticut.

By the end of that summer in 1969, my first summer in Connecticut, Barbara came to visit with her sister Nancy. Barbara was working in Indianapolis as a dental hygienist, and we developed an active relationship, both by phone and letter. I felt so good about her and about us. When my dad met Barbara, he told her, "You are better than the others."

Ann was a former nun and a friend of the Copelands. A mutual friend encouraged us to date, thinking we were the perfect couple. But I was already seeing Barbara, so I introduced Ann to Bob Luther, and they fell in love very quickly. Barbara ended up moving into the apartment above Ann's mother's when she moved to Connecticut later that year.

Leaving The Marianists and Marrying Barbara

Jesus said unless you die for my sake…..

I had hoped I could stay in the priesthood and have a family, but there was no path for that. I had to follow a process once I decided to leave the Catholic priesthood. Fr. Darby had become the President of the Superiors of all the Roman Catholic men's religious orders in the US and moved to Washington, DC. He was replaced as Provincial Superior by Fr. Ferree, a great scholar and researcher and an authority on Fr. Chaminade. When I decided to leave, I went to Dayton to meet with him. I shared the story of why I thought I should leave. He wasn't unkind but was persistent that I was making the wrong choice. He told me I was deciding on the side of wisdom, but I had to decide on the side of will. He didn't lend himself or his mind to feelings of love.

I could have simply left the Roman Catholic Church, but I wanted to receive a dispensation from my vows. I had come in the front door and wanted to leave by the front door. I wrote a letter to the Pope in May 1969 and explained that I felt I was being called to marry and have a family. I wanted to impress upon him that my mind and heart were fully open to the calling of having a wife and could not retreat from that. French Cardinal Sepie was responsible for reading all the letters from priests who wanted dispensation. My request protocol number at the Vatican was 2,310. That meant there were over 2,300 priests ahead of me who wanted to end their vows and be free to marry, and those were just the ones who had applied for dispensation; many had simply left. That was quite an astonishing realization. Later in life, someone told me that there were hundreds of former priests just in the Denver area who left the priesthood, most without the dispensation.

I went to Pittsburgh to visit my parents after writing to the Pope and read the letter to them. My mom was very put off by the letter; my father was not surprised, but he didn't say much.

Barbara

Barbara— it was certainly her person, but also it was her faith that attracted me. That is what made the choice easy.

I went to visit Barbara and her family at Christmas in 1969. I asked her parents for permission to marry Barbara and explained that I planned to leave the Roman Catholic priesthood and request dispensation. I proposed to Barbara in Dayton at her family home.

I went to see Jane in Cornell before Barbara and I were married. Jane was involved with a psychologist there; he seemed like a good choice for her. He was stable, had a stable life, and was a nice guy.

I had been waiting for months to receive the dispensation from the Pope. Barbara and I had decided to marry in April, as we thought that would give enough time to receive the permission. But it didn't come, and we had to postpone our wedding.

At that time, Father Vasey was stationed in Rome as an emissary from the Marianists to the Vatican. I decided to send a night letter to him as my friend and superior to ask him to intercede for me with the Cardinal. I expressed to him that I was in 'moral jeopardy'; I had taken a vow of chastity, and that excluded marriage and intimacy. I felt that if I married without the dispensation, I would be breaking my most sacred vow. To send the night letter, I had to call New Haven to dictate, and the woman actually gulped when I read it aloud.

Father Vasey said he was not at all surprised. He knew me and the way my mind and heart were always reaching out to others. In seminary, I would often foster friendships and saw the importance of relationships. He considered seminary the school of love and thought

I was at the head of it. In hindsight, I find it interesting that he could read me so well, even when I was young. He recognized that I always put my heart above my head.

As previously described, Fr. Vasey was a fiery, conservative, red-headed priest from Philadelphia. Apparently, he went into the Cardinal's office with guns blazing to get my dispensation. Father Vasey called me later that month to tell me that I was free to marry. I had made my appeal through the Archdiocese of NY, but I didn't realize that the letter of dispensation was on a slow boat to America. So we trusted in the word of Fr. Vasey, and Barbara and I were married in June, but it wasn't until the fall that I was called into the Diocesan office in NY. The staff member read the letter that was sent to the office, and I told him that I had already been married in June. He demanded to know which priest performed the ceremony, but I wouldn't give him the name. What stood out to me in the letter was that there was no mention of not having permission to continue dispensing the sacraments—I had emphasized in my own letter that I was not turning away from the church. So I continued to celebrate communion with those around us.

What makes me sad is that years later Fr. Vasey was assigned to the University of Dayton; he was a canon lawyer and assigned to the Marian Library. I was in Denver then, and the kids were young. I didn't know he was assigned there, and then when I did, I wasn't able to go visit him. I should have gotten in contact with him, but sadly we lost contact with each other.

Barbara and I were married at a Jesuit Retreat house in Ridgefield, CT, on June 28, 1970. That morning, I read Isaiah 62. I was powerfully moved by verses 4 and 5:

4. No more will you be known as 'Forsaken' or your country be known as 'Desolation'; instead, you will be called 'My Delight is in

her' and your country 'The Wedded'; for Yahweh will take delight in you and your country will have its wedding.

5. Like a young man marrying a virgin, your rebuilder will wed you, and as the bridegroom rejoices in his bride, so will your God rejoice in you.

This was so directly related to my relationship with Barbara and in line with my soul. My marriage was in line with Him, and our marriage was a union with Him.

It was a beautiful wedding. My family came to support and celebrate us. The morning of the wedding, my father took us all to breakfast: my parents, aunts, siblings, Barbara and I, her parents, and sister. My friend from North Carolina, Fr. Cranor Graves, celebrated the wedding, and the priests from St. Mary's also joined in.

Our Wedding day; With Bill Copeland, my best man

We spent our wedding night at the Plaza in New York City. Then, the next morning, we traveled to Cranor's cottage in North Carolina for our honeymoon. We went again the following year after our son Jay was born. I was swimming in the ocean and got caught in a riptide. I thought I was going to drown; I was really struggling, and I kept calling out to Jesus, and I yelled to Barb to go for help. She told me to put my feet down! I didn't realize I was in shallow water. I came to the shore and was so exhausted I fell to the sand. She asked, "What can I get you?" I asked her to bring me a glass of bourbon.

After our engagement, Barbara had moved to Stamford, Connecticut, and had an apartment. She was a public health dental hygienist and went from school to school to give talks. Dr. Peter Yannity, a dentist, was the head of the parish council at St. Mary's Catholic Church in Ridgefield. Before Barbara came to Connecticut, I told him that she was a dental hygienist. He interviewed her and hired her on the spot.

When we got married, I moved into her second-floor apartment. We had a couch and our collector's cabinet, which we purchased for $500 in North Carolina on our honeymoon. Barbara continued to work for Dr. Yannity after we were married. His dental assistant quickly became a good friend of Barbara's and was a bridesmaid in our wedding.

Jim Brown, my friend and former assistant, was so angry and hurt when I decided to leave the Marianists that he wouldn't speak to me. We had worked closely together, and my leaving was very hard on him. We didn't speak for years until I returned for a reunion with the Marianists in 1974. Specifically, it was a reunion for the Marianists who, like me, had left the order but remained close. During that reunion, we spoke, and he realized he had to forgive me.

Our Early Years Together

When I left the Marianists, what would I do?

I interviewed with the Vice President of American Express to entertain clients and was offered a job, but it didn't pay enough to support us. I then interviewed with a headhunter company, and they offered me a job. But I excused myself because I realized I didn't have enough industry knowledge.

I knew with my education and background that I wanted to stay in Christian education. I heard from a friend in Cursillo, Jack, about an opportunity at St. Mary's Catholic Church in Ridgefield. His kids were in the education program and his son Jay played at our wedding. Jack told me about an opening in their education program, and I had an interview with Father O'Connor. We hit it off, and he wanted to hire me immediately to run the education and train the teachers. The salary really wasn't enough to support us. I remember driving and contemplating what to do, and I heard in my mind, "Seek ye first the Kingdom of God and all these things shall be added unto you." Father O'Connor would later bolster our income with meals, paying for weekend getaways in New England, and so forth.

Father O'Connor was like a big teddy bear who also rode a motorcycle. He had been a chaplain at the Battle of the Bulge in Germany and housed the wounded in the local church. It was a very difficult experience he carried with him; he didn't speak of it, but you could tell he suffered from PTSD. He became a surrogate grandfather to our children as they came along, mainly our first two, Jay and Jeff.

At home with our first baby, Jay

At St. Mary's, we had around 1,200 kids in the education program, ranging from first grade through junior high, and an additional 200 in high school. We divided the whole town into six groups by age. Ridgefield was a town of about 5,000 people, and half of them were Roman Catholic. Barbara became a teacher in the Catholic education program, and she taught a group of kids at our home in Ridgefield.

I worked with high school kids and their parents. We had classes for the kids in the upper loft of the parish center on Sunday nights. We talked about their faith and what they were going through, creating a space where the teenagers could express any doubts about their faith. There were some parents that were part of CUFF—Catholics United for the Faith. It was a very conservative parents' group that would spy on our talks and what the kids would say and then report it to the Papal Nuncio in DC. It would drive Father O'Connor crazy; they were very critical of him and the fact that we were not orthodox in the teaching and sharing of our faith.

It was rewarding but strenuous work. I was responsible for ordering all of the materials and for training the parents. I would work with the parents and their own children in the elementary and middle school groups three times a week. Then I would teach the teenagers on the weekends. The idea was that the parents would learn the subject matter and teaching methods and then continue the program in their homes with the neighborhood kids. I used a series of catechism books, and every child and parent received one. It was a very successful program, and Fr. O'Connor was so happy I could do it. It took a lot of energy, but I enjoyed it.

There were some college students from Fairfield University who volunteered and became a part of the education ministry. They taught the younger kids, including our son Jay, who was now three or four and very precocious. They were really fine young men and continued helping us for a couple of years.

We held retreats for the high school kids in the summer at the parish house. Father O'Connor moved out of the house and into an adjacent building during the retreats. For the last retreat of the summer, Barb said, "You stay home with Jay and Jeff; I'm going on the retreat" – she was 8 months pregnant with Ryan. She stayed in the parish house and used that for the retreat.

When we lived in Ridgefield, the Vice-President of Haagen-Dazs ice cream attended our church. At every church picnic, he brought enough ice cream for everyone.

A British couple at St. Mary's was moving and wanted us to buy their house. It was outside of town in the hills on Aspen Ledges. It was a really nice Cape Cod-style home with two bedrooms, a living room, and a dine-in kitchen. We made the arrangements and bought the house; it also had an apartment that we rented out to a teacher.

During the year we lived there, Barbara and I started a business selling Christian education books and Christian artwork, which we called Sage House. We invested heavily in this business, going to exhibits in New York City and, with Bill Copeland's help, created a catalog for prospective buyers. A German-speaking lady from church helped us in the store, managing it while Barbara was pregnant with Ryan. The school books for St. Mary's were bought through our Sage House business.

Our Sage House Adventures

We saw a one-story house for sale and went to inquire. It was a beautiful ranch-style house, with a big garage we could use for a showroom, and we thought we could handle the mortgage. We renovated the whole downstairs and added an apartment with a separate entrance, knowing that the additional income would be very helpful. We rented the apartment to a young female teacher from the school. We called the home Sage House. It was situated on over an acre of land with beautiful trees all around. Every once in a while, we would run into a copperhead snake. It was located on Route 30 at the bottom of a hill. During snowstorms, when people couldn't get up the hill, they stayed with us. One night during a bad winter storm, we had 11 people stay, including the managing editor of Reader's Digest. We had a big living room, and everyone stayed on the floor and couches.

It was at this house that we had Brandy, our Saint Bernard; she was our first pet. We couldn't figure out why Brandy didn't eat more, especially for being a big dog. But we later found out she went from neighbor to neighbor to be fed. We also acquired a duck at Easter and kept him in the bathtub, which he soon outgrew, so we released him into a lake near the home of the church secretary. Later, when we would drop by the home of the secretary and her husband and go down to the water's edge, the duck would come to the shore to visit us.

It was while we were at Sage House that Ryan was born, and it was here that Jeff fell off the counter while in his baby seat. It was a real shock to us. To this day, we don't know how he fell and how he wasn't hurt. We thanked God for protecting him.

Having fun at the circus in Ridgefield with the three boys

We were cooking ribs one night, and they caught on fire. We tried to put it out but it only made it worse. John Mitchell, a parishioner at St. Mary's, was a friend and a fireman, and he responded to our call to the fire department. Jay was a little guy and was so disappointed that John didn't hatchet down the door instead of us just opening it!

We got to be friends with our neighbors, including a woman across the street and a couple up the road. We went on a day trip together to the safari park in New Jersey. At one point, when we were driving through the park, I looked in the rearview mirror, and a rhinoceros was charging the back of the car. It came very close to running into us but suddenly peeled off. What I later learned is that rhinos can't see at a distance, so when he got close, he realized the car was not a threat in his way.

On the other side of our house, going up the hill, was the O'Toole family. Jim was a psychologist, and his wife was a banker. We became close friends with them. The O'Tooles had twin daughters, and their oldest boy, Jimmy, was the same age as Jay. Jimmy was really talented and precocious; he stuffed potatoes in their toilet once and clogged it up. We were also close to a young lawyer and his wife. She had been the photographer for our wedding.

My primary income at the time was my work at St. Mary's, but it wasn't enough, so I was always looking for ways to supplement it. Through an acquaintance, I connected with a group that wanted me to teach in-home classes on St. John's Gospel. For a while, I traveled in the evenings to a meeting place in Chappaqua, New York. During our second fall at Sage House, my mother came to visit and traveled with us on a trip to Maine.

I became friends with a priest at a Roman Catholic church in Norwalk and worked with some of his adult Christian education teachers. We would sell him books from the Sage House at cost, but in exchange, I gave talks and received a stipend. We had a similar arrangement with other churches in the area.

I continued to work for St. Mary's, but Fr. O'Connor got a new assignment from the Diocese, and his replacement didn't think I should be paid to train the teachers and run the education program. There was a woman who filled in when Barbara and I went on vacation, and she told the priest that we weren't doing enough to be paid. Barbara and I went on a two-week vacation to visit family, and the priest didn't send my paycheck to the house while we were gone. When we returned, I called to inquire about the paycheck, and he said he wasn't going to pay me or employ me anymore. I was livid. He finally agreed to pay me, but that was the end of my work at St. Mary's.

We visited Barbara's family during our vacation

Eventually, we went bankrupt; we couldn't make enough to cover our expenses. We didn't have money to pay for a bankruptcy attorney, so we went to the local library and filed the documents ourselves. We had to put our beloved Sage House up for sale.

Throughout these stop-and-start events, I always knew that God was with us. Barbara and I continued to pray and put our trust in Jesus.

Through God's providence, Barbara got a job in New Canaan working as a dental hygienist. We moved into a big white rental house in New Canaan. Barbara was pregnant with Barrie, and when she woke during the night craving food, I simply walked across the street to the grocery store.

One of Barbara's dental patients was the owner of Weed and Duryea, a lumber company in New Canaan. She told him I was looking for a job, and he offered me an interview. I was hired as a salesman, and he gave me a starting bonus that I would earn through sales. His company had hardened wood that was long-lasting, but when I met with builders, they would complain that it was too hard to get nails through. So part of my job was to convince the buyer of the added value of the lumber. I was making sales but not enough to cover the prepaid salary. I would take Jay and Jeff with me to job sites to sell the lumber. During one of these trips, I was distracted by the boys in the back seat and rear-ended a car at a stop sign. Thankfully, no one was hurt.

In the New Canaan house, the three boys' bedrooms were on the top floor. It was two flights into the house and two flights up to the bedrooms. When we came home late at night, I'd have to carry each boy. I told them, "Someday, you will be carrying me upstairs." I told them made-up bedtime stories about being a missionary in Africa. We developed a garden. I called Jeff and Jay the sod boys – they helped dig up the yard. When Barrie was born, Pop Pop and Nini (Barb's parents) came to visit. Her father, Aaron, helped in the garden and took Jay to school when he started kindergarten.

When we were at Sage House, a neighbor across the street was a photographer. After Barrie was born, he took her photo and sold it to a company that used it for the cover of Baby Talk magazine. He also took photos of the three boys for stock photography. It was a funny thing to walk into stores in town and see the boys' photos in frames for sale.

With our growing family, we needed more income, and I was always ready to take on another job. While living in New Canaan, I sold alarm systems for a time and had to drive a long way to try to sell them. At one point, I met with a family that was considering our alarm system, but they didn't think they could afford it. When I went back to call on them a week later, their house had been severely damaged in a fire. I also sold windows for a time.

While we were in New Canaan, we started attending a charismatic Episcopal church in Darien, and Barrie was baptized there. Terry Fulham was the rector and a great biblical scholar and preacher; he really believed in the presence of Jesus in the Eucharist. Eventually, the Associate Priest told me, "Jim Short, you should be an Episcopal priest."

I went to see Terry Fulham, and when he learned of my background as a Catholic priest and my desire to continue to minister, he became my ally. I asked if he could get me an appointment with an Episcopal bishop to be an Education Director in the diocese. He introduced me to the bishop in Dallas and then to Bishop Frye in Denver. The bishop in Dallas wanted to hire me, but Bishop Frye was more inviting. I knew about Bishop Frye through the charismatic renewal. He was very charismatic, and I was excited to meet him.

On my way to meet Bishop Frye, I stopped in Detroit to see my sister Jeanne. She was in the hospital, and it was really shocking to see her since the last time I had visited. She had an aneurysm, and they had a helmet on her head to alleviate the pressure. She had several pieces of medical equipment connected to her to keep her alive. She had been my nemesis as a child, but as adults, we were friends. She wrote me a beautiful letter when I was ordained and came to the first Mass I celebrated in Mt. Lebanon.

I prayed with her and had her say the Apostles' Creed, and she professed her faith in Jesus.

I stayed that night in the home of a priest friend and woke up early in the morning. I heard the phone ringing and knew it was for me. Lee had come in the previous evening and visited with Jeanne. When I answered, Lee told me that Jeanne had just died. I felt good that both Lee and I had gotten there before she died, and I knew she had faith and was home with the Lord.

Moving To Colorado

When I spoke with Bishop Frye by phone, he said he didn't have any employment for me but invited me to come to Denver and join the Diocese of Colorado. My meeting with him was really positive; he was very interested in hearing my story of becoming a Roman Catholic priest, my decision to leave to marry, and the work I had done at St. Mary's for the Christian Education program. I went to an education meeting for the Diocese and met Fr. George Castano. He was very involved with a Sunday School scripture curriculum he had created, called "Living the Good News." I stayed with him, and he told me more about it. Upon hearing about my education with Lumen Vite and Fordham and my experience at St. Mary's, George felt that I should run the program. I went to Bishop Frye and asked if I could find the funding; could I assume directorship of Living the Good News? He suggested a few wealthy donors in Colorado to contact. But when I reached out to them, they had all gone to Arizona for the winter. I didn't get the funding and was greatly disappointed.

I was looking for a bishop who believed in me and would provide a future. Even though I didn't have a job, I felt that Colorado was where we were supposed to be. We moved out of New Canaan, and Barbara and the kids went to stay with her parents in Kettering, Ohio. We were really stepping out in faith. I went to Colorado and stayed with Fr. George for two months. During that time, he provided me with housing and meals without charging me. But then his sister came to visit. He was the baby of the family, and she thought I was taking advantage of his hospitality. She told him to ask me to leave, and he did.

During that time, I met Lucy Pritchard, who was at St. Philip and St. James Church (aka PJ's) and served on the Bishop's council. Lucy was a very smart and elegant woman and also very charismatic. She was funny and fun. She and the parish of PJ's took an interest in Barbara and me.

The Diocese, at the urging of Lucy Pritchard, invited me to come and give a talk to the Executive Council I went and they said they didn't have the money but were interested to hear about "Living the Good News." I presented my ideas for the curriculum and told them it would be foolish if they didn't start it. Fr. George's idea was so creative, and I felt incredibly enthusiastic about the potential of the program. The teaching was organized from preschool to adults. It pulled from the liturgy and the readings for the day. But it was also an action-oriented curriculum. It had an instruction and a theme for the season (Advent, Epiphany, Lent, etc.) and included an activity at the end where each of the levels would come together to present their activity (whether it be art, a song, etc.). It magnified how the Sunday teaching could be expressed in an artful way. I knew we could develop it into something great. After my presentation, they asked me to step out so they could discuss it. When I returned, they said they had a property in Capitol Hill they could sell to fund the program, and they wanted me to run it.

This was a real turning point in my and the family's life. I was so excited to tell Barbara the great news. I went to get Barbara and the kids in February of 1977, and we drove from Ohio to Colorado. In Kansas, we got stuck in a dust storm. When we finally got to Colorado, we didn't have enough money for food, so I went to sign up for food stamps. I was dressed nicely, and they served me first. Looking back, I suppose I should have been embarrassed, but at the time I was just grateful. We relied on those food stamps over the following months until I officially started with the Diocese.

Jay, me, Ryan, Barrie, Barbara and Jeff in Colorado

Once I started with Living the Good News, it was great to have a steady income. It wasn't a lot, maybe $1200 a month, but it was enough to get started. We rented an apartment in nearby Lakewood, where Jay started first grade at a local school and Jeff started kindergarten. The lady across the street from us saw that Ryan and Barrie didn't have shoes; she bought them each a pair.

While we were at the apartment, some kid threw a rock through the window, and it landed in Barrie's cradle. Thankfully she wasn't there. It was in that apartment where Ryan fell off the washer in the kitchen and banged his head. We always took those things in stride with the kids. For instance, while in Connecticut, a family invited us to their home for Thanksgiving dinner. We had a nice dinner, but Jay pushed Jeff into the fireplace, and we had to take him to the hospital for stitches.

We soon moved to a duplex on LaSalle Street in a cul-de-sac. Jay was riding a bike, and it was Jeff's turn. There was a street next to the house that went downhill—a good place to learn to ride a bicycle. We put Jeff on the bike, told him not to look back, and I let go. He kept going! He didn't fall and did great.

The National Air Guard station was nearby, and they practiced parachuting drops on a field near us, which was very exciting. I remember there was a snowstorm on Halloween, so I bundled up toddler Ryan, put him on my shoulders, and took him out trick-or-treating. He got blanketed in snow and looked like a little snow bunny.

We started attending PJ's on Sundays. There was a guy who would teach classes on Terry Fulham's sermons. He was a trainer for United Airlines, and was also an expert skier. He would take our boys to the mountains to ski and would take turns skiing downhill with one of the boys on his back. Each Sunday we were invited to someone's home for dinner and to watch the Broncos' games. This was the start of our Bronco fan hood.

Dennis Callaghan, who I had met through the Marianists and became a friend, came to visit us during this time; he was out of money then. He asked if I could lend him some money. I only had $20 and gave it to him.

We befriended a guy who was living on the street, and he stayed with us on the couch at our home on LaSalle. During the night he would help himself to the food in the refrigerator, and eventually, we realized he was a grifter. We told him he had to find another place to stay; it was too crowded.

Sometime that spring, I received an invitation to visit an Episcopal church on University Avenue that was very akin to the Roman Catholic Church. The rector had heard about me and invited me to come and join his parish. But when I heard him talk, it didn't resonate with me; he was very conservative and hadn't changed from the old

Catholic liturgy to the Vatican Council changes. I knew it wasn't a good fit, and I wouldn't last there long.

When we first started working on Living the Good News, we were based out of an office at the Diocese. We took over storage areas and the auxiliary room or any space available. We were using the Diocese's printer for everything, and we had people coming in to help us. Our presence soon became disruptive to the routine of the Diocesan staff; Fr. Christopher, the Bishop's assistant, became very annoyed with me. Whenever Fr. Christopher, would complain I would go to the Bishop, and he would smooth things over with Fr. Christopher.

There was a young couple that came to the Diocesan Center; I think she was hired by the Diocese. But we enlisted her help, and she wrote the commentaries on the scripture for the Sunday school teachers to be used each Sunday. There was a gentleman at PJ's who owned a plane and Bishop Frye hired him to fly me around the Diocese. I visited different churches within the Diocese looking for curriculum writers, and we advertised the program to all 30 Diocesan churches. The goal was to encourage all the Sunday school teachers across the Diocese to provide material for the seasonal lessons. We had a team of editors that would review and sharpen the material.

We produced the first edition for Advent, Christmas, and Epiphany and printed 330 copies to distribute. Meanwhile, we advertised to non-Episcopal churches, including Catholic, Lutheran, and Presbyterian. So for the next edition, Lent, we had orders for over 550 copies. When we reached 500 copies, the diocesan copier couldn't handle it. Max at the print shop in the Diocese was a young layman at the time, and later became a priest. He was a very nice guy. We would literally lay hands on the printer to pray over it, and it would start up again. When we got to the Summer edition, we were producing over 1000 copies. We limped along until we decided we could get it printed professionally.

We moved from the Diocesan center to Epiphany Church on Colorado Boulevard, where I was hired as a part-time assistant to the priest. It quickly became clear that it wasn't a good fit and we should not stay. We then moved to the Church of the Ascension; they had a basement area that was devoted to storing food for a food bank. But there was plenty of space for us, and the church paid for the necessary renovation. We had an office, an assembly room, and a meeting area. Wherever we went, we found people to help with the writing. There was a lot of goodwill, even if it wasn't always great writing—it required a lot of editing and rewriting. I hired a very good editor, Vasiliki Eckley, whose family was Greek Orthodox.

There was a lot of printing and collating, and we needed people to help—our kids even helped collate the editions. We wanted to get people in the diocese involved to help with the writing. Barbara and I took over the adult education part of it and worked late into the night on the curriculum. She once famously said, "This is a man killer."

During our short time at Epiphany Church, we met Mike and Carolyn Spence, who became our good friends. When we wanted to move closer to Denver and my work, we found a house on Newport Street, near Ascension's Gilpin Street location. Mike was a lawyer and handled the closing and co-signed the mortgage for us.

Newport Street was a great home for us. The boys attended Wyman Elementary, and they picked Jay to star in the musical program.

I was traveling to different churches to present the curriculum. On one occasion, I was invited to present to the Christian ed people in the Diocese of Western Indiana at a church in South Bend. After talking about the program, I was invited to meet with the Bishop. I went in to talk with him about the program, and he interviewed me for a long time. He was incredibly enthusiastic about the curriculum and my work with it.

In the summer of 1978, Ascension asked me if I would fill in for the priest who had left the church, Fr. Bob Burrows. As part of my work, they asked me to set up the curriculum for the Christian Education and Sunday school.

Over the summer at Ascension, I really looked forward to giving the sermons. I talked about the gifts of the Spirit and praying in the spirit, and no one objected. They started paying me a substitute priest income, and that really helped; we didn't have to live so hand to mouth. Barrie was a toddler at the time and became popular as she waddled around the parish hall.

In the meantime, I was on my way to my second interview at Trinity Church in Peru, Indiana, at the invitation of the Bishop of South Bend. He had extended a formal offer to be head of education for the diocese and rector of a parish. Peru is where Barnum and Bailey housed in the winter, and the boys were excited about that.

Before I left, I met with Bishop Frye, and he asked me to meet with him again when I returned.

When we went to the airport to fly to Chicago, Bishop Frye and his wife Barbara happened to be immediately ahead of us to board the flight. Bishop Frye said, "I hope you have a good time and that you hate it." I told him I would meet with him when I returned.

Indiana was really appealing to us because it meant we would be a lot closer to Barbara's family in Ohio and my family in Pittsburgh. We had a great visit. The church really welcomed us; we had dinner and met with the parish council and people involved in the education program. We went on a tour of the parish home we would live in; it was quite large, everyone would have had their own bedroom, and it even had a phone booth. They even noted that the kids could join in a Barnum and Bailey camp during the summer!

While the invitation to Indiana was very inviting, I kept my promise and met with Bishop Frye after my return. I shared what we had learned and the reasons the position was very appealing. We were in the chapel next to his office, and he prayed over me. He prophesied over me that God was saying, "I want you to stay where you are and be part of the Diocese in Colorado." I decided to stay in Denver. When I called the Bishop in South Bend, he was very disappointed and upset with me.

Meanwhile, I had told Ascension about the offer in Peru. Carl Wells, the Senior Warden, went to Bishop Frye to say that the parish at Ascension wanted to hire me; they had already posted a call to hire a rector for Ascension. I had served as the interim priest, and the Diocese had a protocol of not hiring an interim rector for the permanent position. But Bishop Frye made an exception, and in December 1978, I was hired as rector of the Church of the Ascension.

I had to become a Deacon before I could be installed as a priest. Once I was hired, everything was taking a long time. At one point, I met with the Bishop and asked when I would become a Deacon. He invited me to attend the annual Diocesan Convention in Colorado Springs. Most All of the rectors and spouses, as well as senior wardens, were in attendance; it was a large audience. I gave a presentation on Living the Good News, and it was very well received. I was getting to know the clergy of Colorado, and it was a great group of people.

When I was received as a Deacon with Bishop Frye

Once I became a Deacon, I needed to take some classes that were specific to the Episcopal Church. One was on Canon Law, which I took at the Diocesan Center. I also had to learn the liturgy of the Episcopal Church and study the prayer book. They wanted me to write about why I thought I could be an Episcopal priest having come from the Roman Catholic Church. I told my story of coming up through the Marianists and how, wherever they went, they emphasized community in Christ. This was demonstrated through the relationships among the brothers, priests, and working brothers; it was all about inclusiveness, and I felt strongly that the Marianist order was akin to the spirit and emphasis within the Episcopal Church.

We had my installation as rector at Ascension in February 1979. When I was hired full-time at Ascension, Helen Barron took over running Living the Good News. At the time, we had over 1,000 subscriptions and had completed the Spring/Easter edition. Helen went into the summer edition and continued to work out of Ascension, and I took on the role of consultant. Vasiliki could have taken over the program, but Helen Barron was already working in the Diocese and proved to have good organizational and business sense. Vasiliki stayed on for a time, but it was awkward as they both were in leadership positions. It was a very busy time; I was ramping up at Ascension, and consulting with Living the Good News. In May 1979, we welcomed our daughter and fifth child, Robyn Sage Short.

All of this was God moving and directing my life. "For I know the plans I have in mind for you," declares the Lord, "plans to prosper you and not to harm you, plans to give you hope and a future." God's words to Jeremiah (29:11) became an important scripture for me.

Beginning with my sister Jeanne's death, over the course of a few years there were nine deaths in the family. During my early time at Ascension, my Aunt Adelaide died. I made plans to travel to Pittsburgh for the funeral, and at the airport, we decided I would take Barrie and just carry her on with me (in those days you could do that). She then lost her shoes on the plane, and I had to ask the stewardess to make an announcement to ask everyone to look for them. They turned up four rows in front of us. When we got to Pittsburgh, my mom and Aunt Mary took Barrie to get clothes for the funeral. Barrie wasn't intimidated by the casket; she actually climbed up on the kneeler next to the casket to look in at Adelaide.

Adelaide was a very dear aunt, my mother's friend from childhood and a very generous support for me getting ready to go to Mount Saint John for prep school (and really throughout my life). Later in life, Adelaide worked at Mercy Hospital as an assistant to the Director. She had Alzheimer's and reached a point where she couldn't function to keep up with the work. Finally, the Director had to replace her. That was a difficult time for her; she really depended on that job as an achievement. She had an active mind, but it wasn't functioning correctly. Adelaide and Mary moved to an apartment in Mt. Lebanon. It was too long after leaving her position that Adelaide died due to complications from Alzheimer's. Mary stayed in the apartment on her own for many years after Adelaide's death.

Ascension

The first day after being received as an Episcopal priest at Ascension, I was in Lakewood and came across a motorcyclist who had been in an accident. I ministered to him in his death. I met with his family and played a part in the funeral service.

As a priest, I very quickly realized that I really liked working with people in a pastoral situation. People come to a church with expectation, with fear, with joy, with a desire for healing, with the willingness to be their best selves, and to find security and peace in the midst of all the disruption in their lives, with a desire to get close to God. I really enjoyed the 22 years I spent at Ascension. I most of all enjoyed helping people come home to themselves and to the Lord; to pray themselves into a new beginning with the awareness that God is right there with them, wanting to speak to their hearts that great Shalom that He said to the apostles the night of the resurrection: "My peace I give you." He holds nothing against us; He only wants us to be our best selves so that we can reflect and mirror His wonderful loving presence in our lives. And I think with that we can throw anything else into the mix (our relationships, work, history, dreams) and see how it all comes out.

The Early Years

Ascension had a rectory located next to the church. We were offered that house as part of my hiring package. I said, "I don't think you would want us living next door. With five young children, we can be pretty noisy." Joe Strickland, an attorney at the church, heard that we needed a house. His deceased aunt had owned a home at 768 Gilpin, just up the street from the church. Joe got clearance for us to buy the house, and people at the church provided the down payment. The house needed a lot of work. We moved in on a snowy day at the end of March, and it was so sloppy with all of the traffic in and out. Peg and Bill Humphrey came and helped clean and organize the house. Jim, a British guy, also helped frequently. He was a character; he had served in the British Army in the Borneo War. He did some work at the church, and then we hired him to work in the house. It took an awful lot of work to strip and restain all the woodwork in the living room. Always up for family projects, the kids pitched in too.

Peg and Hump really took us under their wing. I stayed with them later when I had my first back surgery. They had a chair lift on their stairs that made it possible for me to get up and down the stairs.

The early years at Ascension were effortless and very supportive. It felt so good; I was quickly immersed in the life of the parish. There were so many things going on.

People from the parish came to our home for different occasions. A group came on St. Patrick's Day, and at the start of dinner I got a call from a priest in New Orleans. He had parishioners in Denver who were at the hospital.

I left the group and prayed in the Spirit on the way. When I got to the hospital, the family was in the room with the daughter, Susan. Her skin was yellow. I said, "Susan, I'm going to ask you some questions, and you don't have to answer out loud (her family was sitting there). Is there anyone that you've held in your heart as hostage?" She burst right out that her previous fiancé had rejected her and was involved with someone else. She was bitter. I asked if I could pray with her and if she was willing to surrender her bitterness. I told her I'd pray that the Lord would help her to forgive. I explained she didn't have to feel the forgiveness but instead to simply make a decision and claim it in the Lord's name. She agreed, and as I prayed, her color returned to normal immediately. The change was so dramatic I thought she was on her way to a complete healing.

I left and returned the next day to check on her, expecting good news. But the family reported that the doctor told Susan the tumor in her abdomen remained and it was the size of a Nerf football. I went back every day for three days to pray with her. Her illness persisted, but she really transformed in her spirit. Susan was married to Jim, whom I met at the hospital, and they had a two-year-old daughter. On Tuesday evening, I asked Susan if she was willing to go with the Lord if He wanted to bring her home to Himself. I asked her what would be the most difficult thing about leaving this world and she expressed deep sadness over leaving her daughter. But her husband was very stable and loving, so she knew he would take good care of their little girl. I read her scriptures, then I told her to imagine herself on a hill where she was looking down into a beautiful green savannah with multicolored flowers. The Lord was inviting her to run down into the beautiful grassy land. She said she was willing, and we prayed together. I went the next day, and Jim was there with her praying the rosary, as he had done each day. She was preparing for her death, and at noon, she died.

It was very powerful; I knew she was ready. She had completely transformed her spirit and surrendered herself to the Lord. A year later, Jim came to visit. He was engaged to a woman who reminded me of Susan. I counseled them, and they were married. Jim and Susan's daughter was the flower girl, and we held the wedding at Ascension.

Ryan's soccer coach, Jessica, had kids the same age as ours and we became good friends. Her oldest daughter was engaged, and I counseled her and her fiancé for their wedding. Not long before the wedding date we discovered her fiancé was already married. I called Bishop Frye and asked what to do. He advised me to call one of the judges in the church. I called two of them and asked for their advice.

Even after learning that he was married, Jessica's daughter didn't want to leave him. So, I invited him to come to the parish office, and she came as well. He was always standoffish when I was counseling them. I confronted him directly, "The jig is up. You are already married. This engagement cannot continue, and you cannot be married here." I asked them to remain and discuss what to do next. But she said she had decided to go with him to his home. I later received a call from his mother saying I had interfered with their plans for marriage. They moved to Maine, and I believe they are still together today.

I stayed close to Jessica after that and officiated at the wedding of her next daughter. Jessica loved to cook and often had us over for meals. I invited Father George along to meet her. I wondered if they could be a couple, but they continued as just friends.

Years earlier, George had married a much younger woman, and they had two children. She was killed in a scuba diving accident with her brother in California. They had been over to our house the week before. The Bishop gave the sermon at her funeral; it was the saddest funeral I had attended. Eventually, Fr. George's daughter Anna went to East High School and played on the boys' rugby team;

when she played, they always won. Sadly, his son went off the deep end as he got older. Anna studied biology and became a research biologist. She tried to bring her brother back on track but couldn't do it. I really feel bad that I didn't get a team that could track him down. I don't know if I could have been a help to him or not. I've inquired about him since, and Anna tried many times to rescue him, but he didn't come around.

Exorcisms

I was drawn into the ministry of exorcisms early on; there were events where I was asked to step up to the plate and bring the power of the Lord to bear on that person. When I lived in Dayton, Ohio, I worked with a woman who was very deceptive. I could see that her life was off track with all the lying, and I really wanted to help, but she wouldn't give me an opening, even though she obviously needed some kind of deliverance. She was in a car accident and ran into a tree and was killed I really prayed for her soul after that. I think sometimes the Lord allows things to happen to people so He can rescue them. I believe He rescued her.

In my time at Ascension, I performed a number of exorcisms and deliverances.

There was a professional woman who, at two years old, witnessed her parents murder their newborn baby as part of a satanic cult. It deeply affected her, and she wanted to help people who were similarly affected. As an adult, she became a professional counselor for people who had been involved with satanic cults. Her own counselor, a Presbyterian minister, heard about me and asked if I would work with him to deliver her from the satanic hold that they both felt remained in her psyche. I assembled a few people at church, including her counselor, and we set it all up, including the crucifix and the candles, and celebrated Mass before she came. When she arrived, she stood at the back of the chapel and called me every name in the book. I listened and then I said, "Ok, would you like to come up, and we will pray for you now?" I told her what we wanted to do. We addressed her childhood trauma and how deeply it affected her. She started to act up, so the minister restrained her, put her on the floor, and we circled around her. She recounted the story, and I told her we wanted to relieve her of that burden. She was not possessed; she was obsessed. It was like a creeping crud deep in her system. That spirit had embedded itself in her soul. I told her that Jesus wanted to free her from these satanic entanglements. I asked if she was willing to be released, and she said yes. As we began to press in and pray, she began to perspire.

At the point where we got her to relinquish the spirit, she let out a blood-curdling cry. She was so infiltrated with the spirit that when it released her, it was extremely painful. My secretary, Pam, was in the office at the entrance of the building and heard the cry. Afterwards, she asked what happened. We then sang a hymn, and when we helped her up from the floor, she was soaked from perspiration. Her whole demeanor had changed, and she left the church to return to her work of counseling.

Another time, the rector of Christ Episcopal Church in Aspen called to ask if I would come and pray for release for a woman in her Bible study that she believed to be possessed. I asked for the woman's number so I could speak with her before making the trip. I explained I didn't want to come if she wasn't willing to let go of the spirit. The woman agreed, so I went, and the rector joined me in our meeting. The woman was an artist and explained that Satan had come to her as an angel of light and inspiration and said if she would accept him, he guaranteed that he would help her develop her art and her business. After two hours of prayer, discussion, and profession of faith, including reciting the Nicene Creed, I asked her very directly, "Are you willing now to join us in expelling the spirit?" She looked at me with dark and demonic eyes and emphatically stated, "NO!" I'll never forget the voice of that "no"; it was powerful and haunting. I realized I wasn't looking into her eyes but into Satan's. When I boarded the small plane for Denver, I was so angry, I remember pulling the seats when I was walking down the aisle. The next day was a Sunday and I was still very unsettled. I sought out Fr. George and Fr. Dave Wilson to pray with me. I shared what had happened and the anger that had overtaken me. I think I was unwittingly wrestling with the devil from my own strength instead of relying on the power of Jesus and declaring His name. I had taken it on as my own personal warfare. In doing so, I opened myself to the devil. They prayed over me, and I was at peace and able to give the sermon. It was a powerful lesson for me.

One Easter Sunday, the usher came up to me and said there was a woman in the back of the church acting crazy and that he thought she was possessed. He asked if I would come back, as we were finishing the service. I asked him to invite her to my office. When I walked into the office, I could smell her from the outer room. I knew the smell as the smell of Satan – something between vomit and poop. I had a few people come with me, and we prayed over her. But it wasn't a complete exorcism. She ended up in Porter Hospital. I got Canon Burt Womack to go with me, and we prayed over her again. Lynn Harkrader from Ascension was a psychiatric nurse there, and she prayed with the three of us. Together, we delivered her from the spirit.

Sometimes a person gets very emotional when you pray over them. Lucy Pritchard at St. James was gifted at delivering people. Deliverance is a lot of spiritual massaging and ministering. When you see someone become successful in that ministry, it gives you courage to step out in faith and have the same success. I always tried to channel God's love. When someone is going through great strife, grief, or difficulty, you can call upon the name of Jesus and share God's love and word to strengthen them and lead them through it.

The Importance of Seeking the Lord in The Midst of Suffering

The thing about being a priest is that you can grow very close to people, brought together by big events; you are invited to be on the inside of people's lives. If you added up all the stories and experiences in the life of a parish, it would be very dramatic. One afternoon, I was out front talking with Bill and Peg Humphrey when a man in our parish arrived and asked if he could talk to me. He had a beautiful family with kids the same ages as ours and had a high-level position in banking. We went inside, and he told me he recently completed a drug and alcohol treatment program and wanted to give his life to Jesus. I was so happy; we prayed together in the office, he opened his heart, and gave his life to the Lord. Then, to my complete shock, Barrie came home from school a few days later and told me that he had taken his life. I think he had known what he was going to do and wanted to be ready to meet the Lord. While this is misguided reasoning, I believe the Lord accepted him. He was a prayerful man and had a really big heart.

There was another man who would come to the church sometimes. He had inherited a lot of money as a young man and had been through many struggles. He had been married to the daughter of Janet, a woman who frequently stepped forward to offer a lot of direction for how things ought to be done in the church and was a great contributor. When I learned that he was an alcoholic and needed help, I went into action right away. He was easy to get next to, and I talked him into going to a treatment program at St. Luke's Hospital. He came to the church one evening to tell me that he had finished the program and had given his life to the Lord. Not long afterward, I was at a prayer meeting at church, and he came in to tell me that he was engaged to be married again and that she had great faith in God. She had influenced him to seek the Lord through scripture. A short while later, they went to Arizona for a hot air balloon ride, and on live television, the balloon caught fire, and they both were killed.

There was another gentleman who had part ownership of the Broncos. He had a lot of money and a farm in Arizona but didn't manage it well; it ultimately caused him to go bankrupt. I learned that he had lost his money and was very despondent. He wanted to take his life so his family could have the insurance money. I made an effort to engage him; I would take him to lunch, and we would play racquetball at the Denver Athletic Club. This was over a period of time. Barbara and I went on a trip, and while away I tried to reach out to him but couldn't get through. When we returned, I learned that he had committed suicide. It was such a shock and so sad. We had spent so much time together in prayer, but he just couldn't see how his family and children had any benefit to him living. They were a beautiful family, and his wife was a gentle, sweet, elegant woman. The daughters were wonderful young adults.

I had another man who phoned me from Hawaii. He and his wife had a home there, and she had died of natural causes during their stay. He called to make arrangements to bring her home. He wanted to have the funeral for her at Ascension. He had a very successful company in Denver, and they had a beautiful family. When he returned from Hawaii, he committed suicide. They must have been in their early 80s; he wanted to be buried with his wife. We held a double funeral. I spent time with their four adult children, and they were such kind and faith-filled people. They were peaceful in the midst of their loss.

There was a young woman at the University of Denver who I had spoken with on a few occasions. I hadn't gotten to know her enough to be able to intercept her intention to end her life I was so saddened when I learned that she had.

The only way to health of mind and body is in giving one's life to Jesus. His name in Hebrew, Yeshua, means He heals, He saves. A person has to go through real conversion and transformation at all levels of their humanity. And I believe that the banker did go through a conversion and commit his life to Christ. But the others I wasn't able to get through. The one gentleman who had lost his fortune was just unable to commit his life to the Lord. He felt like such a failure and believed his only redemption was to benefit his family through his own death and therefore life insurance. He believed this was his financial way of caring for his wife and daughters.

This all happened in the span of a couple of years, and it really wore me down. I was incapable of saving them. I clung to the belief that God wanted every baptized person with Him. Jesus said, "I will never leave you or desert you." That is very powerful to me. I think love also plays such an essential role. I think even in their moments of death, they carried the love that their families and I had for them.

Best Things About Being the Rector of a Parish

At the altar at Ascension

I think being the rector of a parish is what I was meant to do: to be with the people and take on the things that were important to them through prayer, meeting with them, encouraging them, commiserating with them, grieving with them, and rejoicing with them through all the things that happen in their lives. It was better than writing the curriculum—though that was worthwhile and something Barbara and I worked on together. I felt like I really settled down and was at home when I started at Ascension. I could get next to people.

People are my greatest enjoyment. The relationships I develop are the source of my greatest joy and my greatest sorrow. After the baptism of the Holy Spirit, this only increased. The Lord brought so many people into my life, and His timing was always right. At Ascension, I mostly enjoyed the people. I enjoyed giving hugs to everyone as they left church and hearing about their lives and what was important to them.

Over the years, I celebrated ~(approximately) 250 weddings at Ascension—270 if you include extended family weddings. That was the most enjoyable part for me: working with couples. We used the Focus Inventory, an ecumenical program developed in Omaha, to help the couple better see themselves and their compatibility. In the midst of that, it was always my intent to find out their faith development and either help them come to a greater or a beginning faith in Jesus.

My intent was to help people come to a deepening faith and love of the Lord. Annie and John Warren belonged to Ascension, and when Annie came home from church, John would ask, "What did Fr. Jim talk about?" Her response was always, "He talked about Jesus." I was never a great preacher; I stuck to professing my faith in the Lord and the importance of our relationship with Jesus.

The sermons I preached at the two Sunday services were important to me. I always prepared ahead of time. The first thing Sunday morning, I would get up early to prepare and refresh my thoughts. During the service, I would pray in the Spirit quietly while sitting and listening to the readings. When I got up, I tried to stay in contact with the Holy Spirit and relate to the congregation. The subject matter would flow from that. Sometimes it took detours.

I recall one Sunday, prompted by the Holy Spirit, I told everyone we were going to take time to find someone else in the congregation with whom we needed to make peace, whether to forgive or ask for forgiveness.

I rarely read a sermon, but I did at the funerals for my dear friends Tom Manion and Jane O'Donnell. There were facts about those two special people, their lives, and my relationship with them that I wanted to get right because it wasn't to them, but rather about them. I spent a lot of time with Tom; he had a very fertile soul; he played the organ and was choir director. He was gay, and we talked and prayed about that. At one point, he decided his separation from his gay partner would serve as an opportunity to deepen his relationship with the Lord. He was a sensitive and cheerful guy. He had an apartment in the undercroft of the church and felt he belonged to Ascension and the congregation. Tom was a real friend to me and to our family, and he typified the expression "a servant to the servants of God." Jane O'Donnell was very involved at Ascension, and she critiqued everything at church. I realized she was a perfectionist. But before I realized that, I got really mad at her one day and said, "Jane, you complain about everything. No one can do anything right." She burst into tears, and I felt terrible. After that, we became very good friends.

I spent a lot of time talking to Fr. Bruce Youngquist, but I didn't know at the time that he was already in the early stages of dementia. He regularly forgot things, repeated himself, and expressed uncertainty in himself. He always had a lot of suggestions for me—too many. After spending an hour talking in my office, he returned to his, but then quickly either came back to my office or called because there were suggestions he wanted to make more clear. As I said, it was a lot of repetition. He didn't want to be an assistant priest; he wanted to be co-Pastor. But he had a difficult time giving sermons because he couldn't remember what he wanted to say. Even when he wrote his sermon, he got it mixed up. There were parishioners who really liked Bruce, including some of the young couples. He took a genuine interest in people in the church, and he wanted to be a good priest for them.

When Fr. George gave a sermon, he had it written down and read it to the congregation. Generally, it was a sermon that he had prepared for the readings years ago when he was a pastor.

Fr. Dave Wilson, who was much more formal than anyone else in our group of priests, became a friend. He had a difficult background in the church; he felt he had been personally attacked by people in his previous congregation and carried those battle wounds. His wife, Dorothy, was a very devout person; they were both faith-filled.

Fr. Bruce's wife, Jo Youngquist, was a wonderful person. Gradually, she became involved with Living the Good News and became an editor. When the publication moved into the city to an office building, she worked there. She was gifted and became Helen Barron's assistant.

Sometime later, when they had moved to the highlands after he retired, Jo shared Bruce's dementia diagnosis with me. Bruce, at one point, was moved into a memory care home, and I visited him there. He would get very depressed, and that was connected to dementia. Jo made sure to tell Bruce who we were before Barbara and I came to visit them. There was a lot of sadness in that. When I learned from Jo how dementia had affected Bruce, I repented for all my annoyance with him and his need for continual reassurance.

Ranald Macdonald figured into church life in a big way. He served as a liturgical and chalice minister. He always had some idea of the way things ought to be at the church. One day, much later on, Ranald had an accident; he fell off a ladder when working in his yard onto an iron fence. His wife, Jedeane, called me, and I rushed to the hospital. I wanted to go into the emergency room with him, but the doctors did not allow that. That was very hard. Ranald didn't make it out of surgery. I stayed with Jedeane to pray for a long time. In the early years, I sometimes thought of her as my adversary. She had a lot of criticisms and suggestions; in her mind, she was always earnest. In hindsight, I see that her input served to sharpen my mind. Jedeane became my good friend after I retired. At the time, she was writing a novel about a couple in Poland.

As the charismatic influence continued to be refined in me, I could see the importance of the realization that God's love needs to be very front and center in our hearts and with one another. The main thing was that we all really loved one another and could live with our differences. And we did. It was pretty darn telling the way the congregation grew closer and always showed up for one another.

Ascension was really perking; many good things were happening. We had home prayer meetings in small groups during Lent. We organized the groups by neighborhood and assigned leaders. The idea was that we would have people praying throughout the city for the duration of Lent. Colleen Barnes had approached me about praying the rosary, so I had a small group that would meet in my office to pray. These prayer groups grew into real support groups, and people shared their lives with one another. It was a huge success. We also supported St. Francis Center (a day shelter for the homeless in downtown Denver) financially and had volunteers there regularly.

What Was Hard

People brought the best and the worst of themselves to church. And they felt free to air their gripes. Working through their personal problems was easy – I wasn't on the defensive, but it got to the point where people felt free to speak their minds about me. The competition about the budget among the vestry was tense. I took a laid-back approach. The members were business men and women, and this was right down their alley. The hardest thing was the infighting. I didn't like that, and there were a couple of people that I could never do right by.

With some people, I addressed it directly. I had some difficult secretaries. Suzanne was the secretary when I arrived at Ascension. She wasn't difficult to manage but was very negative. Every morning I came in, and she was in a bad mood. I said to her, "Suzanne, I find it very difficult every morning that you are in such a foul mood and you project that on me. I need you to brighten up." And she did. She was all about goodwill. We became good friends. But she and her husband had their own kind of prejudice and ideas. They sang in the choir, acted in the plays, and all that was positive. They were basically good people. But her husband was part of the team that was very critical of me and thought I was heretical for bringing Mary into the fray (through my trips to Medjugorje, praying the rosary, and so forth). In the mornings, I would come into the church and say good morning to him, but he wouldn't answer me. I had to learn to be friendly and open-minded toward people who were critical of me. Gradually, most of them became my friends.

Early on in my ministry, I had Dianne as a secretary. Dianne wanted to be a spiritually accomplished woman but was so steeped in her own spiritual misguidance that she projected that onto me as a rector. She would tell lies about me to parishioners. When I realized what was going on, I said, "Dianne, your job is to support the rector. The lying that you do about me, and apparently your desire to see me leave this calling, is very destructive. What I'm asking you to do is simply stop talking negatively about me to the parishioners, and if you continue, I'm going to have to ask you to please leave. Because it is not helping Ascension and the congregation." There were weird things that happened. One day at a staff meeting, she came in and told us that a man broke into her home the night before and attacked her; but something about it just didn't seem to ring true. She was very bright but filled with anxiety and conniving in her deceit of people. I asked Leonard, a parishioner who volunteered in the day-to-day operations, to help me work with Dianne. I really felt that the devil was playing on her psyche. So we planned a deliverance and asked her to meet with us in the chapel. In talking with her, we unveiled the predicament that she was in both in mind and soul. She was very defensive and began to play the role of someone occupied by spirits in her voice and manner. This was really early on before I had much experience in exorcisms or deliverance. At first, we broke her down, and then we tried to bolster her and reconstruct her confidence in God. I don't think we really helped her. With no great surprise, she began to talk about me again. So I told her she had to go. After some time, she came back and threatened to sue me and the church. She had wanted to get her doctoral degree in Theology. Bob Gill, as Senior Warden, decided that the church would give her the money rather than go through all the difficulty of a lawsuit. I think it was upwards of $10,000. But that offer seemed to quell the attack mode she was in. I think she got her doctoral degree. I can't remember where she applied. I always hoped that her education would really help her. I really believe that was great discretion on Bob's part. This was very early in my ministry. When I reflect back, I should have seen the signs. When she first started, she told me she didn't want me to pray in the Spirit with her.

I used to eat lunch occasionally at Angelo's Restaurant. Nancy, a waitress there, lived in an apartment above the restaurant. She was always very friendly and helpful, and I didn't know she was addicted to drugs. One Saturday, I got a call from Nancy: "Fr. Jim, I want to stop taking drugs, and I want to give my life to Jesus." I said, "Well, you are on the right track." So she came to the church, and we prayed. She was a very talented woman and was skilled in graphic design. Sometime after that, I hired her to be my assistant and to do design for the events we were promoting. She was very good at her work, truly overqualified, and I really liked her. Very often, we would have spiritual conversations, and she would rise to the occasion of whatever it was.

After a couple of years with us, she decided she needed to go back to New Jersey, where her life and her addiction had begun. That was difficult because she was a very good person and employee. It's interesting; when someone gets away from an addiction, they become very fruitful in their ministry. And she caught on to the mission of Ascension to help people grow closer to God.

There were always challenges, but there was also so much good that was happening. The flow of the Spirit throughout the church was strong. We used Rick Warren's materials for building the church and for the vestry during Lent. There was a lot of good flowing in.

I began to have people get up and talk at the Adult Education class on Sunday mornings. I invited people to speak, including Bill Dorn, Janet Whitlock, and Jane O'Donnell, and they gave magnificent testimonies about their faith and how they came to know the Lord. It was very fruitful, and the person giving the talk was bolstered by their own witness. Parishioners really liked it because they connected with the personal element of the testimonies. We did that for at least a year. I met with the person ahead of time in my office and asked them to tell me the story of their faith—negative, positive, fearful, challenging, whatever. I then gave them suggestions for how to turn it all into a positive witness, and that seemed to help. I had all kinds of parishioners give their witness, and it had a very positive effect on the congregation. It showed that we accepted people as they are and watched what God did with them and for them. Those witness talks led up to Lent and the things we did at Lent with the prayer groups.

We wanted to absorb people into the parish by projecting joy, health, and a positive spirit. We found good scripture books to use during Lent one year. The leaders met in the education room upstairs. During that time, Jack and Becky Fles got married on a Sunday afternoon and we danced the night away at the reception in the parish hall. Our kids slept until 2:00 PM the next day. Jack was our youth leader. While our youth program was strong under Jack's leadership, the Cathedral sent their teenagers to us, and later on, when they had a strong youth director, we sent our teenagers to them. That is how Jay got involved in Young Life, a scripture-based ministry for teenagers where they shared their real-life outlook and experiences. He went to California for Young Life and also to Lake Powell.

Later on, I hired Thomas as Youth Minister. He wanted to be a priest. He didn't have great judgment, and I tried to explain what was wrong and help him along the way. We had to sponsor him in order for him to go to seminary, and I told him I wasn't ready to commit to that until he could show better discernment. I really worked with him. Some of the things he did were good, but it always was in fits and starts with him. He did eventually go on to seminary.

Over the years we had several street people that would come in for assistance. We would provide financial assistance but I also really worked to relate with each of them and show them God's love. It was a challenge because I didn't always know who the person was that

I was dealing with. There was one guy that would often show up when we had a special event or retreat occurring. He was sort of a threatening spirit and I often wondered if I needed to have the police present. The police were always very responsive if and when we needed them. But many of the people that came in were good and I felt like we built a connection.

My secretary Pam had her office by the accessible day entrance to the church. I told Pam we wanted everyone who came to feel welcomed. We would try to usher them into the chapel to pray with them. We also offered them coffee and sometimes snacks if we had them. One lady that came had little children and my heart went out to them. So one day I decided I was going to go to her home to see her in action with the children. I discovered that she was on drugs and the money that the church provided for the care of the children was being used to purchase drugs. When she came again with the children I confronted her about her drug abuse and we stopped giving her money. I would give her food when it was available.

Wanda was a native American woman that would come to meet with me who I really liked. She invited me to come and visit with her and her mother, Phyllis. Her son was a nice young man and a talented artist. He gave me one of his paintings of Jesus' agony in the Garden of Gethsemane.

I really sought God's discernment and to share His love with everyone who came into the church.

Overall, my time at Ascension was very positive, but there were definite sinkholes along the way.

Trouble At Ascension

For some of the congregation, I became an obstacle. The very people I treated well and tried to be good to, and to be especially close to, became my nemeses.

It was a real leadership kind of congregation. I didn't feel the need to micromanage. I wanted the vestry to oversee the business side of the parish so I could focus more on pastoral care. We had a group of successful young businessmen who were accustomed to running the show. They began to vie for control among themselves, and they would have intense discussions about the budget. Gary Johnson was part of that group on the vestry. He contributed a very significant amount in tithing each year, and he felt this meant he had greater discretion on how his tithing was spent.

Of course, all that gradually built up. About ten years into my ministry at Ascension, four of the 12 members of the vestry decided among themselves that it was time for me to leave. They said, "We appreciate all that you have done, but we think it is time for new leadership." In the meantime, the priest who was the rector at St. Luke's in Fort Collins invited me to be the assistant and heir apparent to be rector. So when I was told some of the vestry didn't want me to continue as rector, I thought fine, if they don't think I'm doing a good enough job, I can accept that. I'll just call the priest to inquire more about his offer. But I decided first to pray; so I went home after the vestry meeting and told Barbara that I wanted to go back to pray in the chapel. I decided to stay as long as needed and wait in prayer until the Lord told me what He wanted me to do. Sometime in the early morning, I heard His voice within me as clear as can be: "It's okay, you stay, and I'll take care of the results." His words resonated in my soul, and I felt very much at peace. I trusted in God's direction and promise to me. I decided to relate to the vestry what I experienced.

So I went back to the vestry at the special meeting the following Tuesday and relayed what the Lord had told me. The vestry member who was the most antagonistic seemed to forget that I had been the Lord's instrument in an intervention for his alcoholic wife. He said, "You're telling us that the Lord is telling you to stay. But we are telling you to go." He got up, shuffled all of his papers, and said, "I'm leaving."

Bishop Frye came the following Tuesday, spoke to the remaining vestry members, heard them out, and then took a vote. Eight of the remaining vestry members told Bishop Frye that they wanted me to remain as rector at Ascension. I went back to the office after the meeting, and Bishop Frye followed me and said, "You know what I think, I think you should leave." He didn't want me to be under the negative pressure. I was so disappointed in his reaction; God had given me the direction to stay.

Shortly after, Barbara and I attended a conference at the Lutheran Church on Alameda Avenue where Bishop Frye gave a talk. He had a magnificently deep, commanding voice and people liked to listen to him. After the talk, toward the end of the evening, his wife Barbara came up to me. I said that was some presentation; she gestured putting her finger down her throat. I can picture this so clearly and it triggered my frustration with him.

When my Barbara and I went home, I told her I needed to go to the Bishop's residence. I went and knocked at the door, and Bill answered. I asked to speak with him for a bit. So he sat on the couch and I paced around the room, telling him there were things about him that really disturbed me. For example, after he supported me in the vestry meeting, he then suggested to me that I should leave. Shortly after the incident with the vestry, he and his wife Barbara came to the Sunday service at Ascension. When I saw him afterward in the Nave, he didn't give any indication of bonding or support for me. It was really disappointing, like seeing an old friend and him not acknowledging you. What occurred to me later on is that his experiences in his childhood family at a young age greatly affected him, and there was something that held him back in stepping out to nourish our relationship. I was really upset and elaborating on what I had come to tell him that night, and I kept circling the living room. I must have been rather forceful because, at one point, he put his arms up as if I was going to hit him. He said to me, "Do you realize you wouldn't even be at Ascension if it wasn't for me?" I said, "I do and I'm very, very grateful." He looked rather surprised, and his expression relaxed. But he didn't extend himself to me at that moment.

What I realized later was that Barbara Frye was upstairs listening to my ranting and was concerned, but it really pointed out something that she knew: that was a big difficulty in his life.

He could come to people's rescue; he had been the Bishop in Guatemala and had come to the defense of the church when it was threatened. He was durable and an enlightened man. But his inability to turn the dial and get on the frequency of the personal relationship was not within him, and that is what I really wanted and worked for. I told him that this weakness in him was very telling. Leaving the Bishop's residence, I shook hands with him and thanked him again. But from then on, he was standoffish with me.

Within a year or so, he announced his retirement from the Diocese and accepted the offer to go to Sewickley, Pennsylvania, to serve as head of the Episcopal Seminary. He sent a letter after he was established there to some people in the Diocese and asked for contributions to support the seminary. I went to our treasurer and said I felt like we should send a stipend of $500, which was significant at the time. I wrote a personal letter to tell him how much he inspired me over the years and how grateful I was to him.

Gary Johnson was a very successful realtor in Denver. His elderly parents had moved to Denver, and I quickly developed a bond with them; I would often visit them and bring communion if they were ill. Gary and I became friends, and he took Jay hunting. He once told me he thought Ryan had the gift of healing. It really impressed me. Ryan actually does have the gift of healing in personal ways; he can smooth over any tough situation. Gary approached me during the turmoil. His wife's parents were also in Denver. They had all discussed it and felt it was time for me to leave. That was particularly hurtful given my relationship as a priest with all of them. All four of the vestry members who wanted me to go including Gary, and their families, left Ascension shortly after I decided to stay.

Sometime later, Gary came to the church. I asked him to come into my office to talk. I told him that if he had spent the same time and energy in giving me feedback to help me to be a better minister and administrator instead of coming after me to get me to leave, it would have been more productive and we would have all benefited.

When a rector is appointed, he or she goes through a lot of checkpoints. By the time the rector is established, it is not healthy for anyone to go after him or her. There is a scripture about this: 1 Timothy 5:17— "Let the elders who rule well be considered worthy of double honor, especially those who labor in preaching and teaching." Faithful elders are worthy of honor, which means we should be slow to criticize and not criticize lightly. And Hebrews 13:17: "Do this so that their work will be a joy, not a burden, for that would be of no benefit to you."

Someone told me during that time that if anyone came against the rector, it would bounce back to him or her; they prophesied that the church would blossom in the next ten years and some of the people that came at me would experience difficulties. I didn't wish for that to happen, but it did for some of them.

Sometime later, I had taken Mark Gill to the DCC to play golf, and we saw Gary Johnson there. He came up to say hello, and I gave him a big hug. Mark wondered how I could do that after my experience with Gary; I told him it was how I believe the Lord wants me to be.

Sean Taylor had been very involved in the exorcism we had done on the therapist from the cult. Sean inherited a significant amount of money from his family. His son had Tourette syndrome, and he would take him to Germany for therapy. Barbara and I had been close to Sean and his wife and really liked them.

But in time, they expressed that they wanted me to divorce Barbara; they thought she was an impediment to my ministry. They didn't realize that she was actually an important inspiration to my ministry. They had also reacted to Barbara's relationship and reaction to Cami, a little girl who we were in the process of adopting and discovered that she had learning differences and attachment issues; they thought it was offensive. Sean was adopted and had a child with special needs, so it was personal to him. On the Sunday before he decided to leave the church, Sean served as the chalice minister; he never gave any indication that he was not going to return.

I often say people bring their best selves to the church and their worst selves to the church. There was a young lawyer on the vestry, and one time at a vestry retreat, he really attacked me. Later that night, he came up to me and said, "You know, everything I said tonight I was saying to my father." People often project their issues onto the priest.

Julie and Dave, a couple who were very active in the church, came up to me on Christmas Eve after the service to tell me that they were leaving Ascension. They were part of a group that really protested that Barbara and I belonged to the Denver Country Club. There was another member who belonged to the DCC as well, and he would make arrangements to have vestry meetings there. We didn't draw on the church for the membership to the club; we used the inheritance from my father for that, and as clergy, our membership fees were greatly reduced.

Richard was an active member of the vestry and a friend. Whenever we had speakers that were different, or not right on the mark of what he thought was true faith, he would tell me that I shouldn't have them, or I should counter what they were saying. We had an Irish singing group come and perform and stay with us. Their music was wonderful and very faith-filled. He felt that their talk was a little off the mark from his more conservative beliefs, and he was concerned. Despite our different perspectives, he was a very good guy and very generous with his time and giving.

A year or so after the push to have me leave, and then the vote and my decision to stay, I went to the vestry to say that we needed more income as the kids got older and started to go to college; I asked for an increase in salary. Some people never agreed to that. When you start arguing about salary, it is difficult, but I just stated what we needed. Some responded to me by saying don't bring your personal problems to the vestry, but others understood. I didn't get too upset by it all; one of the women on the vestry who objected didn't have any children and was only looking at the business side of it. I stood up at the annual meeting and shared that I decided that during the next couple of months I would not take any income from the church. I fasted for a couple of weeks, taking just water and crackers, and took the opportunity to go visit Tommy Tyson at the Aqueduct Retreat Center in North Carolina. Occasionally, Tommy Tyson came to Denver for a conference or to speak at Ascension, and he stayed with us. Tommy had been a meat packer in his younger days and was a stocky guy with a big, deep voice; Jay called him Tommy Tough Guy. He was so supportive of Barbara and me and made a big fuss over us when we would visit. When I shared with him my troubles, he confided in me about his own troubles and people wanting him to leave. We had a shared experience and grew closer during that time. He was truly a source of cleansing water during a difficult period. When I returned from North Carolina, I spoke with my friend, Dennis Callaghan, about what was happening at Ascension. He sent us money, which kept us afloat during that time. I just continued to trust in the Lord, and the following year I did get a raise and a bonus as a way of bolstering our family.

The thing about me, my strength and my weakness, is that every relationship is personal. A personal relationship doesn't mean a sexual relationship. I had a personal relationship with everyone. When it involves the other sex, it can get confused or misunderstood.

When I went to Medjugorje the second time and saw Maria's face after her visit with Mary, I was floored by the love and light reflected on her face, and I was struck by the power of Mary's love. This really influenced me and my ministry. What I learned to do was to love each person that I worked with. I learned to pray and ask for discernment in my relationships while also treasuring them. This was essential—the heart of my ministry.

Barbara felt I was too open, too friendly, and too accepting of people. But I found that everyone needs acceptance, and then you work from there. I felt that a priest must be understanding and caring to be effective.

When I sat down with someone, I asked the Holy Spirit to enlighten me and guide me in what I said and how I reacted to them. If I really listened and was open and when needed, apologized, then it allowed for the relationship to heal or grow. This approach is not something I was taught in seminary nor in my previous work but rather something the Lord led me to.

When I told Bishop Frye early in my ministry that the one thing I had trouble with was divorce and remarriage, he said, "The one thing I've decided is that divorce from marriage is not an unforgivable sin." I learned over time that some marriages can be healed through groups like Marriage Encounter, but some cannot be repaired because they are too destructive for the partners involved or because of an unwillingness to change on the part of one or both of the marriage partners. Even in my own family, I learned that some marriages are unhealthy for the person experiencing it all. With my daughter Barrie, I was the last one to hang in with her marriage to Matt, but I came to the realization that their marriage was not good for either of them. I realized that while reconciliation with the Lord and with one another is at the core of Christianity, not every marriage can be healed. Even more personally, Barbara and I sought counseling when we reached stumbling blocks in our marriage. Our counselor, Jay Brenneman, was a very gifted counselor, and he told me that I was too demanding of our oldest son Jay and in my relationship with Barbara. In general, I had a controlling personality, and I had to learn to let go, both in my relationship with Barbara and my relationship with the children. You think you see the more perfect way in a relationship, and then you try to mold it to that way of being. But I learned that everyone has his or her own way of understanding their part. And I learned to ask God "Lord, what in me needs to be corrected?" If I wasn't defensive and really was open to what the Lord needed to change in me then it really helped. You really do have to let go and let God.

The Second Ten Years at Ascension

There was a group in Evergreen, Colorado, called the Episcopal Renewal Ministry that helped churches discern and strengthen their ministry. They traveled the country and gave talks and workshops. They came and held a workshop at Ascension.

When I began to have trouble at Ascension, I went to spend time with them; they prayed over me, and I was deeply affected in the Spirit. The head of the ministry predicted that the next ten years of my ministry would be full of the love of the Lord. It was very encouraging at the time and proved to be correct. Those ten years were a very fruitful time and my best years at Ascension yet. While we had lost a number of families, we survived and thrived. The essence of charismatic renewal is love. Jesus commanded, "Just as I have loved you, you must love each other."

The head of the ERM wanted me to travel with him to Texas to accompany him on his talks and healing sessions. He was very charismatic, had a lot of gifts, and a very strong and gentle spirit; but it wasn't the right time.

It was during that time we started the Alpha Program. Alpha is a faith development program that started in England in 1977 and developed over the years until it was finally taken over by Nicky Gumbel, an Anglican priest from England, in 1990. When we got hooked into Alpha and Nicky Gumbel, it really sparked the Spirit of the church. It helped many get past their religiosity and hang-ups about religion. He was a good influence. He said you could say anything you wanted about what you did or didn't believe, but you couldn't attack another person for what they did or didn't believe. This really was God-like and helped a lot of people heal and create a much more loving community at Ascension.

We held a number of retreats in the mountains for Alpha. I wanted people to tell the story of their life and how God had influenced them. It wasn't always a clear point for those who had grown up in the church. It wasn't always dramatic, and the stories and their experiences really varied. But to hear each of their individual testimonies was really gratifying and stimulated others to think about their own journey.

The man who owned the retreat center was a little harsh, but his wife was very nice. We weren't great at keeping to a tight schedule—when we went to bed, got up, and ate meals. He would get very frustrated with the lack of a strict schedule. I told him that the things he was objecting to weren't that serious and tried to explain why it needed to be more free-flowing. It was stressful for me to try to navigate with him, and after a couple of times, we didn't return to the retreat house.

Years later, I drove past the retreat house with Judith Muller to spill Tom's ashes over the mountainside, and it brought back many good memories. It had been a place of blessing for the church and was a beautiful location.

For several years, during Lent, we hosted Seder dinners to observe the Jewish celebration of Passover. We invited Rabbi Urbach to come and give a talk each year. Hump and Peg prepared the meal in the kitchen. One time, the rabbi talked for a very long time, so Peg and Hump stayed in the kitchen and kept reheating the soup. Unfortunately, they also kept drinking. They were great but were 'slightly altered' by the time the meal was served.

At one point, we saw a spike in crime in Denver, specifically murders. We decided to host six different prayer marches throughout the city during Lent. We enlisted the help and support of pastors of various denominations to join along with their congregations.

We met to pray in front of the Catholic Cathedral, the State Capitol, and different churches in areas experiencing surges in crime. We then marched to specific locations where crimes had been committed. Dave Gill was my assistant at Ascension at the time and served as the cross bearer for the marches.

The first place we went to was our own Episcopal Cathedral. On Easter Eve, we went to a location known for regular drug dealing. The Denver Post covered the event, took a photo that included Barrie, and it was their front-page report on Easter morning. The marches were a powerful and ecumenical experience, and, as later reported by the Post, the crime rates declined during that time.

As I've shared previously, my sermons did not always follow my original plan. One time at church, Fr. George was sitting with his daughter, Anna, and I could tell he was embarrassed. Anna had dyed her hair green! I announced that we were going to have a hair contest and the congregation would vote by applause. First, they voted for me and clapped a reasonable amount. Then I had them vote for a bald gentleman. Everyone laughed and clapped a bit. Then I asked Anna to stand up, and everyone gave her a big round of applause. I think that helped George feel more relaxed.

Cami

Friends of Children of Various Nations (FCVN), an adoption agency, had an office upstairs at Ascension. We were close to them and often contemplated adoption. When Robyn was six, we determined we were ready. They placed Cami with us when she was five years old, and she shared a bedroom with Barrie and Robyn. Cami was Korean and had been moved between a number of foster families before she came to us.

Early on, there was something about Cami that didn't sit well with Barbara, and it was difficult for them to bond. We would travel to Evergreen for counseling sessions. Barbara would hold Cami in her lap; it was very difficult for Barbara because she had the feeling that Cami wasn't the right fit for our family. She was very smart and could be manipulative. Cami would periodically ask me, "Will you always keep me?" I would reassure her. We traveled to Pittsburgh one time, and my brother cautioned me that she may not be the right child for our family. My brother was always very intuitive.

We brought in a specialist for learning disabilities, and they discovered a few challenges, including an attachment disorder. Cami had been through a few foster families. The woman who was doing the therapy once a week for Cami in Evergreen had told us that Cami would need therapy into her 20s. Financially, we weren't prepared to do this, as it was an expensive service. But I figured if God wanted something, he would provide the means.

I was determined that we were going to keep her. But it became obvious that we could not do that. In total, she was with us about a year. Barbara felt a sense of relief and peace; I was heartbroken. I was taking a shower and wept heavily, knowing I would have to break my promise to her.

FCVN told us that they had found a family in Evergreen that could take her, and they had previously adopted two boys in their mid-teens, with the same learning differences and adjustment challenges that Cami had. The husband was the Vice President of a bank, and they could afford the counseling and therapy Cami would need. When I found this out, I ran from the church up the street to tell Barbara.

Jeff and Jay were our moral compass, and they were very upset when we shared our decision to give Cami up to another family. It was similar to when we had gathered the children together in the living room at 768 to tell them we were going to get divorced. Jeff and Jay got really angry.

Early in our marriage, Barbara and I would go through verbal battles; a lot of it was when we were living in Aspen Ledges in Ridgefield. We weren't getting along. Barbara felt like she was in competition with God for my time. It happened again when we were in Denver. As a rector, there were so many demands on my time and attention. There were times when church demands conflicted with our family plans, and I felt it was my obligation to be present to the congregation. One of those times was when we had planned a family vacation, and a young couple in the church had a child die. I struggled with the decision to stay with the young couple for the funeral or to travel with my family. The couple was very close to Fr. Bruce Younquist, and I thought he would be a good choice to stay with the family. But they were so upset that I wasn't going to be there. It was mainly the church that was the source of our issues or tension between Barbara and me. She would take on people in discussions in the church; one time she even took on Bishop Frye in a meeting.

I never accepted nor believed a divorce would happen, but I couldn't convince her of it. So I thought I would let it all play out. It was only when she told the boys we were getting divorced and they became so angry with her that she changed her mind.

Our disagreements were also often about Cami. Barbara really struggled with Cami, and I would take up for Cami or try to temper Barbara's reaction. When we told the boys of our decision to give up Cami, their reaction didn't change our minds. It was a difficult decision but the right one for our family, and ultimately the right one for Cami as well.

Balancing Family and A Ministry

Barb and I had our own relationship, and it had highs and lows. I would never take it to the point of seriousness that Barbara would; I would just try to mend my ways where they needed to be "mended." Every couple has those kinds of troubles, especially young couples. I tried to give primetime to our family, especially around the holidays and on trips. The road trips were a big part of our family life and bonding experiences.

On the trip to Mexico when the kids were little, we played Neil Diamond songs and sang the whole drive down. We went to a natural swimming place with rocks. I think the trip to Ryan's college graduation was a real together time. All the trips brought us together and were exciting. The things that really helped us bond as a family included our trip to Mexico, our summer trips to drive east to visit family, our summer in Singapore, our travel to Medjugorje, and my sabbatical to the UK.

My advice to families is to travel with your kids. When I was growing up, we never went on a family trip. I think when families go on trips, especially long-distance, it really brings the kids and the parents together.

During our trip to Medjugorje

Back Trouble And Retirement

"We also carry around in our body the death of Jesus so that the life of Jesus may be revealed in our body. For we who are alive are always being given over to death for Jesus' sake, so that His life may be revealed in our mortal body." 2 Corinthians 4:10-11

The condition of my back is a story in itself. All back problems have an origin. Mine began as a 15-year-old playing soccer at Mount St. John. A twist and a turn did the job. It was not serious enough for medical attention. I just lived with it and tried to take it easy for a while.

What I found out much later on was that somewhere along the line, arthritis had developed at the site of that injury in my lower back. Finally, after years of mild flare-ups, a parishioner at St. Philip and James Episcopal Church, where Barb, the children, and I attended, asked me if I would help him move a piano into his house. What I didn't know was that I would be on the bottom end of the piano going down a rather steep flight of stairs to the basement, using every bit of strength. My main objective was to not let the piano run over me. I pictured the cartoon where the coyote was chasing the roadrunner and often got flattened. I was holding on for dear life.

Years later, we were donating a piano to the church, and I carried it out to the garage with Jay; we also moved a refrigerator. It was definitely my "strength" to move. As a result, my first back surgery in the mid-90s helped to correct some of the problems, but not really. As I was leaving the hospital and deciding to walk from Presbyterian

Hospital to home, the surgeon warned me not to fall. He said if I injured my back again, it would require a more extensive surgery.

Sure enough, many activities with the children as they were growing up demanded a lot of stamina on my part. Gradually, my back began to suffer. I repeatedly tried deep massage and acupuncture. Meanwhile, continual demands at the church kept me on my feet and on the road.

In the early spring of 2000, I had been counseling Danielle and George Wilson (Jen's brother). I had planned to do their wedding and traveled to East Hampton. But in the days leading up to the wedding, I decided I just wasn't able to officiate because of my back. We called in the priest from Christ Church in Sag Harbor to fill in. During George's wedding, I stayed home with Julia, my first grandchild, who was an infant at the time. When Julia cried, I would pick her up. One time, I experienced a spasm in my back while I was holding her; I yelped, and she just turned around to look at me with a look like, "What is going on?"

When I flew home to Denver, I spent most of the time in the galley talking with the flight attendants. It was too painful to sit, so I stood for most of the flight.

During what turned out to be my final summer at Ascension, I had scheduled eight weddings. After the first three, I realized that I couldn't fulfill those commitments. It was very painful for me and very disruptive for the couples. My desire was, through counseling, to help couples work through wrinkles in their relationship. Using the FOCCUS inventory from a company in Omaha, the 152 statements that the couples separately answered flushed every important issue to the surface in their relationship. I would work with the couples for as long as it took (and they were able) to work through those points. One of those couples was Nancy and Joe Yeaman. Nancy was a very engaged, insightful, and spiritually tuned member of the church. I was so disappointed to not perform the weddings, and some couples really got mad. I hated to not continue, but I just wasn't physically able. Nancy did have her wedding at the church, and when she arrived, I was sitting in the office and felt embarrassed because I looked fine. But I wasn't fine. I was on my back most of the time. I had to pull myself up the steps to the church.

That summer, I performed a wedding for Ann Wilson, Jen's cousin, in East Hampton. Jay was my acolyte, and I asked him to just keep me standing. There were times he literally was propping me up. My back was so bad that I had to lie down after the service in the sacristy.

I was supposed to baptize my granddaughter Julia the next day, but I was not able to do it because of my back. The Copelands came to East Hampton and took me and Barbara back to their home. They helped make arrangements to meet with a top surgeon in Connecticut. But our insurance company wouldn't approve the out-of-state care and instead arranged for me to take a medical flight home.

It became clear that I could not continue to work, and I wrote a letter to the parish at the beginning of the year, telling them that I would retire.

I retired from Ascension in May 2000, after nearly 22 years at Ascension. The church threw a big party at a hotel in Denver. It was a beautiful evening, and there were so many people there whom I appreciated and to whom I was grateful for their love and support over the years. It was an emotional and gratifying evening.

My retirement party with Pam, my assistant and friend, Barb and another parishioner

We moved from our big house in Denver to a retirement community in Heritage Bend. Margie and Clint donated a golf cart to us. We had a great time driving it around the neighborhood and on the golf course. Sometimes we would attach Willie (our Saint Bernard) or Mack (our English Mastiff), and they would walk ahead of us. We had coyotes that would come up on our deck and eat the dog food at night. One afternoon, we had walked down the street, and at the end of the cul-de-sac was a coyote. Mac, who was very big, and the coyote, which was big enough, had a standoff; neither barked nor moved. It was really wild.

We were at Heritage Bend for a little over a year. It wasn't a great fit for us. It was a small house with no guest room. Additionally, it was not a great fit for us in terms of the community and our neighbors. Meanwhile, Jeff and Amy had moved to Portsmouth, VA, to begin her residency at the Naval Hospital, and Jeff was beginning seminary at Regent University. We decided to move to Portsmouth so we could support them and help care for our grandson Harrison. So we made plans to move in September 2021.

Earlier that year, 2001, someone suggested that I go to see Dr. George Frye, an orthopedic surgeon at the Spine Institute of Colorado. He was an experimental surgeon who had trained at the University of Chicago. Dr. Frye had told me that there were no openings; he was scheduled for surgery for the next two months. I called the office, and his secretary wanted to be helpful. She told me that there was one cancellation, and it was in two weeks. The question was whether I could be ready for surgery with all the pre-surgery tests. So I began immediately to prepare for what would be a 10½-hour surgery. The surgery involved taking bone from my pelvis and using it along with synthetic discs, which he would insert into the lower lumbar area. He used titanium rods to hold it together. This was the first of a number of surgeries that would construct a trellis that stretched from my pelvis to the base of my head. Dr. Frye did the first two surgeries, and the third would happen later in Norfolk and focused on my neck.

It happened that I had a wedding scheduled in Aspen for a couple just prior to the surgery. I happened to sit across from another orthopedic doctor who, along with Dr. Frye, had been written up as the top orthopedic surgeon in Colorado that year. I told him what Dr. Frye was preparing to do. He said, "You know, I wouldn't do that surgery. It is too risky. I think another surgery that is less invasive would do the trick." But I was so confident in the training and ability of Dr. Frye that I wanted to go with him as my surgeon.

Prior to the surgery, I asked Dr. Frye if he prayed; he said, "I couldn't do what I do without praying." And I felt safe in his hands. An anesthesiologist who would keep tabs on the action in my body as he got close to the spinal nerves would accompany him. People at Ascension had prayed with me, so I felt confident going into the surgery.

On August 22, 2001, I underwent the surgery. Our special friend Carl Williams came to the hospital and sat with Barb during that very long day. After the long day of surgery, I finally came into consciousness in the ICU, already beginning to experience terrible pain in my back. I was moved from the ICU to a room where I was in recovery for several days. It was excruciating pain as recovery continued over that period. Any movement would ignite a spark in my back that reverberated pain throughout my body. I would scream bloody murder whenever I was moved in any way. At first, the whole floor of nurses and medical staff would come rushing to my room. After a while, they got used to the screams and didn't respond, but would wait me out.

About 10 days after the surgery, because I experienced so much pain, the attending physician ordered an x-ray. Two strong-looking male attendants came; I said to them, "When you move me, I will probably scream, so please excuse me." These well-experienced guys moved me so quickly I only had a momentary flash of pain. And I didn't scream. I was so grateful to them. They took me on the gurney down to the x-ray and got me back in bed.

I had a night nurse during that time who would mock me and mimic my pain. She would say to me in a mocking tone, "Oh, the poor baby, it really hurts." After a while, I got so fed up and angry with her that I told her I had never had a nurse like her; she was so mean. She broke down and cried. She then told me her story. Her daughter was in prison on drug-related charges, and she was taking care of her little grandson. She didn't have much help and didn't make much money. I prayed with her, and after that, we became friends.

During that long stay in the hospital, Barb had to travel to Portsmouth, Virginia, to meet the movers and supervise the unloading of our furniture. I had asked Jeff to choose a house and take over the negotiation of the purchase and closure on the home. The house he chose was on Breakwater Drive in Portsmouth, and out the backdoor, catty-corner across several houses, was his and Amy's home.

Jay had come to Denver with a friend for a visit and to attend a Bronco game. I was still in the hospital, and he had gone down to the pharmacy to get my medicine, including OxyContin. The Oxy would help with the pain, but it definitely made me a little loopy.

Robyn had also come home from NYC, where she was working, to help me after my surgery while Barbara was away.

In the midst of that time, the 9/11 attacks on the Twin Towers occurred. I had just started being able to get up and walk. I made my way, with help, to the cafeteria across the hallway. I walked in, and on the television, I saw the first tower in flames. I was there watching when the second plane flew into the other tower. I felt the need to pray, so I asked the nurses and medical staff; a group of six of us gathered in prayer, along with Camille Vaughan, who had come to visit me. She had brought a box of donuts; I couldn't eat them, but the staff enjoyed them.

Jay hadn't been able to get a flight back to NY, so he rented a car and drove back. Robyn ended up staying in Denver after 9/11, only returning to pack up her apartment sometime later.

I was in the hospital from August 22, 2001, until September 15, 2001.

A great blessing was given to me when a couple from Ascension and our small group, Kurt and Alison Thompson, invited me to convalesce at their home in Wash Park, which had an elevator. She was a urologist, and her husband was in a wheelchair. During the time that I spent with them, they went through the process of adopting a little Chinese girl. She was beautiful and a pistol.

So for two weeks, I stayed with them until I was well enough to take the flight to Virginia. Carl gave Robyn use of his car.

Eventually, I began water rehab at the Broncos facility. Robyn would pick me up and take me to the appointments.

After a couple of days, I could use the elevator to get to the kitchen for breakfast. Robyn would make sure that I had meals. Initially, following my surgery, I had asked Pam, my secretary, to make an announcement to the church that it was very difficult for me to have guests. But a week before leaving their home, I asked Pam to invite people to come and walk with me around the neighborhood. It was so nice to be out in the open air; it was a beautiful fall. Visitors during that time were mostly Robyn and her boyfriend Matt, Camille Vaughan, and Margie. They were very solicitous, helpful, and prayerful. That was a great encouragement. Stephanie Johnson came a few times and would walk with me, and it really cheered me up; it was good to be engaged in conversation with her and focused on her rather than my own pain.

Another person was Bob Miagrossi; he was the junior warden at Ascension. He had told me if I ever needed help, I could call him at any time at all, even in the middle of the night. The anesthesia always wreaked havoc on my system. I called him at 11:30 one night and told him that I really needed help. So he came and took me to the hospital. I had been constipated for nearly two weeks. When I was cleaned out and got back to the house, I was absolutely frozen. It was late September. So they loaded blankets on me, and I slept. I experienced so much kindness and thoughtfulness throughout my recovery.

The plan was that when I could travel, I would fly from Denver to Norfolk. Robyn used her miles with Continental to get me a first-class ticket so I would be more comfortable. It was November of 2021; when I landed at Norfolk Airport, Barbara was there in a beautiful Ford minivan she had purchased from a nice couple at St. John's.

During that time, Jeff was a seminarian at Regent, Amy was an intern with the Naval Hospital, and Barbara was in law school at

Regent. I remember being enormously lonely in bed recuperating. I had been so intimately involved in so many lives at Ascension and with so many close friends. I was grieving the loss of Ascension. It was so hard to move, to get up, and out of bed. During that time, I would take Harrison in his stroller, and we would go around the neighborhood. I would point out colors to him, and he would repeat them. He was such a smart little boy.

Dr. Frye said he was in medical school with a doctor in Virginia Beach. He told me to go see him when I arrived in Virginia. When I walked in, the first thing I said was that I wanted him to renew the prescription for Oxy. It was what had been keeping the pain at bay. But he said no; he wouldn't prescribe it anymore. So I went off of it cold turkey and didn't have any side effects. That was one of those times that I really felt God was taking care of me.

I had a hip replacement in 2002 in Virginia that was also successful.

I came back to Denver for my second back surgery for my upper lumbar. It only took six hours. Dr. Frye put in synthetic discs, two vertical titanium rods, and one across. I was in the hospital for about a week. Carl got me a reservation at the Marriott so I could go down in the elevator to eat and walk. Dr. Frye became a good friend to me.

Along the way, I had neck surgery with a doctor in Virginia Beach. He was a specialist in the region and put in the screws in my neck. It was extremely painful, and the pre-surgery treatment was immensely painful as well. But he was very good. After the surgery, he came in and put out his hand. He was checking my grip. So when I squeezed his hand, he looked at Barb and gave the sign of "phew." as he knew the surgery was a success. Barbara and I really liked him; he was a nice young guy.

A few years later, I was raking leaves in Appomattox rather vigorously, and I cracked a rod and a screw in my back. They were titanium, so that was hard to do. Rather than going to the hospital in Lynchburg, I went back to Denver. Carl met me and went with me to see Dr. Frye. When I saw him, he said, "How on earth did you crack that rod and screw?!" So I had another surgery to repair that.

As I went through these various physical challenges, I would continually pray and turn it over to the Lord. I think it is all about our intention as we go through difficult situations. I would ask God to use my difficulties to help someone else, to make it all worthwhile.

When I was in the hospital, meeting with doctors and receiving visitors, it was all an opportunity to express my faith and to pray with and for them. When I was recuperating in Denver and people would come and walk with me, it was a great time to express joy and faith in the Lord. It was all about being aware of the presence of God in these moments and seeking to use them to glorify Him. I did then and still often sing: "To God be the Glory, to God be the Glory, to God be the Glory forever! Amen!"

St. John's In Portsmouth

2 Corinthians 5:17: Therefore, if anyone is in Christ, he is a new creation. All of this is from God, who reconciled us to Himself through Christ and gave us the ministry of reconciliation.

In 2 Corinthians 5, we are told to be God's ambassadors of reconciliation to God and to one another. Reconciliation is what Jesus was offering when He appeared to the apostles after His crucifixion. He announced Shalom to the apostles, which is the word for healing and reconciling peace. Jesus said, "My Father works even unto now, and I work." The job of the Christian is to be that extension of Jesus to the world.

This scripture is my whole sense of why I'm a priest. Helping people be reconciled to God and then, in turn, to be reconciled to one another is my mission. But people really only achieve reconciliation when they experience God's unconditional love.

After moving to Portsmouth, we visited St. John's Episcopal Church, where Jeff and Amy were attending. I immediately felt very much at home and inspired during the Eucharist. I remember being very emotional that first time we visited; it really felt like coming home to a church. I felt the Lord's presence and true worship. The music, the spirit of welcome, the interest in us as a family— it was so refreshing to my soul, particularly having been away from Ascension.

I had been attending for a few months when Fr. Ron Greiser asked me if I wanted to work as a Pastoral Assistant. It was April of 2002. I got involved with counseling for weddings, visiting the sick, and visiting the elderly and shut-ins. I really enjoyed all of that. I got to do all of the pastoral roles that I loved without having any of the administrative burden. Ron asked me to attend the Vestry meetings in an unofficial capacity. It was an ideal semi-retirement. I also led a Wednesday morning Bible study on St. John's Gospel, which always inspires me. The group was really receptive to me, and we grew in our relationship to the Lord and each other.

One Friday afternoon in Portsmouth, I was going to visit a woman in her late 80s who was scheduled for surgery. I told her there was a crucifix in each patient room at Maryview Hospital; I talked to her about trusting in Jesus that He would bring her through. He did, and when I went to visit her the next time, she acknowledged God's provision.

The week before, I had been rear-ended by a kid in stop-and-go traffic. The EMT insisted that I go to the hospital. They took me to Maryview and did x-rays, and I was fine, but it took several hours.

This was when Barrie was living in DC and coming for a visit that Sunday. We had plans to go to dinner and a movie. I was assigned to preach at St. John's Sunday morning, but I felt done in by the events of the week, and I didn't want to go. I heard the Lord say to me, "Practice what you preach." I had been telling the parishioner to counter her belief that she wasn't going to make it through the surgery. And here I was thinking I wouldn't make it through the service. So I got up and preached and made it through the whole day.

On another Sunday morning in Portsmouth, as I was on my way to church in my clerical clothes, I stopped to get gas at the Getty Station. While I was pumping gas, a man came up and said, "I just murdered a guy." I asked him what happened. He explained that he had a gun in the car and a guy walked up to his car window, pointed a gun at him, and demanded money. His wife and baby were in the car with him. He reached down, got his gun, and shot the man. I explained to him that technically he didn't commit murder; he killed in self-defense. I encouraged him to go to the police, but he didn't want to do that. For once, I had a good excuse for Ron for being late to church.

I enjoyed working with Ron. After experiencing so much opposition from a small group of parishioners at Ascension, I was very much inclined to be on Ron's side when he was in his own battles with the congregation. I felt it was very important to support Ron and show him unconditional love. I always try to see the good in the other person, even when I'm feeling under attack. That is what I instinctively brought to Ron, and I believe he was receptive to that.

There was a prayer group that I led. There was a very nice woman in the group who was very enlightened but who felt that Ron was not truthful. It was concerning to me that she was questioning his core rather than his ministry. I tried to get them to pray for Ron and to see the good in him and how God was using him in a very positive way. It was clear to me that Ron was a true person and a good priest at heart. He would go out of his way for people.

We spent a little less than five years at St. Johns. I developed close relationships with many in the congregation. I was so well accepted and so well called upon for many things during my time there. I felt the congregation was really receptive to the grace of God. I really relish the role of being a pastor and naturally fall into the role of pastor with a great sense of compassion for people. I really felt that they took me to heart, and I took them to heart. I really experienced and also tried to live an unconditional love with the people of St. John's.

Appomattox

Barbara and I read in the newspaper about a property in Appomattox with a three-bedroom house, ten acres, and beautiful mountain views. It sounded appealing, so we decided to take a look at it. It was a beautiful day, and the view really was incredible.

The man next door owned the house; we spoke with him and agreed on the price and details that day. I believe we bought it for $115,000. My position at St. Johns had ended, and the taxes in Portsmouth were high. We felt it was a good move for us financially, and we were both excited for a new chapter. We spent a lot of money to improve the house. We purchased a kitchen from Habitat for Humanity. We added a front porch and a deck onto the back porch. We got so much enjoyment from sitting out on the deck and watching the sunset between the two mountain peaks.

We went to St. Anne's Episcopal Church and met the priest, Fr. Mike; he was a retired army chaplain. We liked the service; it was a small country church. I soon began to help out, assisting with the services and visiting the sick.

We really enjoyed walking in the park at the Appomattox Court House. That became the place we would visit to walk a couple of times a week. Ryan would come from Richmond to visit with Ella, and Barrie was able to visit from Portsmouth.

We had my 80th birthday party there, and nearly 80 family members came. The kids helped with the service and a nice meal at the church. We also had a bounce house and picnic at our home. It was such a fun weekend.

After celebrating the Eucharist at my 80th Birthday Celebration

At our home in Appomattox with Pat, Barbara, our kids and some of my

nephews and niece

Barbara found Rosie at the grocery store and brought her home. Throughout our marriage, Barbara, and later Jay, would often bring home strays. Rosie was the sweetest little Dalmatian dog. No one claimed her, so we kept her. We soon got Murphy and Finnegan. They were feral dogs, and they liked to get free and roam the area. But we always recovered them. The only time they would get close to me is when there was a big storm.

We loved walking in the park; we had some good neighbors, and we liked the people at St. Anne's. The couple next door, Frank and Linda, became good friends. I think we were in Appomattox for about eight years.

As a former Catholic priest, I discovered there were a few former Catholics in the church. Our neighbor Frank was a former Catholic and disillusioned with the church. I remember having a very long conversation with him outside the post office. Eventually, he was confirmed by the Bishop.

We were trying to hire a new priest at St. Anne's. I wanted to hire an Indian priest. He was very smart, very spiritual, and ready to come. We had gotten a very good recommendation from the rector at his church in Northern Virginia. But there were people who didn't want to hire him because he was too dark-skinned and had a thick accent. I was so upset about that.

I also became very involved with the Democratic Party while we were there. I began to canvass for them and for Obama when he was running for President. People were strongly opposed to Obama coming to visit. I remember we knocked on a gentleman's door, and he came charging out with a gun. I said we were there to talk with him about Obama and said "peace, peace." He retorted that if Obama won, there wouldn't be any peace. Barb had backed off the porch when he came out, and we quickly left.

The kids were pushing us to move to a bigger city with easier access to a medical center and an airport. So we ultimately ended up moving back to Denver.

St. Luke's Church

We moved back to Denver in November 2015. Our neighbors and friends, Frank and Linda, helped us move across the country. We moved into Windsor Gardens, and Ryan and Josh, my son-in-law, helped carry the furniture up to the fourth floor.

We were looking for a new church home, but we knew we couldn't return to Ascension. A retired pastor becomes like a fifth wheel in their previous parish. So we started attending St. Luke's Episcopal Church, where Ryan and his wife Whitney were attending. Ryan was teaching in the Sunday school program, Godly Play, a great program in the Episcopal Church that engages children in the lessons through play and creativity. Ella and Kate, Ryan's daughters, were in his class on Sunday mornings, and they would come to the sanctuary at the time of communion.

Barbara and I have remained at St. Luke's these past ten years, and we really like the congregation. I continue to be involved with Bible study groups with members of the parish. As time went on, individuals in that group, other members in the church, and previous friends and connections in Denver became my ministry. I also continued to work with couples in preparation for marriage, many of whom were extended family. That attention and ministry continue to this day.

Shepherding Through Death

"I have loved you with an everlasting love, and now in my tender mercy, I draw you to myself…"

I used to say that I felt like an usher to death: "this way, please." It was one of my greatest satisfactions to be with people in their dying because I could direct their minds and hearts to God. I couldn't even begin to count the number of people I've ministered to in their dying, but there are a number of instances that stand out in my memory where God was truly glorified.

There is one experience that stands out in my spiritual development when I just had to stand up and do what I had to do. Early in my time at Ascension, I received a call from an elderly woman asking me to go with her to Park Manor, a retirement center. Her friend Elizabeth, a militant atheist, was dying. When we entered the room, the first thing I said was, "Elizabeth, your friend has told me that you are an atheist and don't believe in God. But I've got to tell you, God believes in you." Scripture poured out of me, emphasizing how much God loved her. When I entered the room, her head was turning back and forth like she was really struggling. But as I talked, prayed, and read Scripture, her body calmed down. It was such a clear sign that she was at peace and settling with God.

I had prayed in the spirit the whole way there because I knew she was tough and would need God. After our visit, her friend drove me back to the church. When she returned home, her phone was ringing as she walked in; it was the attendant at Park Manor, and he said, "Elizabeth has just died."

Jim Blair was a doctor in Denver, and I visited with him and his wife, Myla, when he was ill; I was with him a lot before he died. Later, I went to be with Myla when she was dying. When I walked in, she was lying in bed and had a beatific look on her face of light and joy; seeing this brought tears to my eyes. She was so completely open to Jesus and died in the Lord with a smile on her face.

Bill Cozar would come to the early service at Ascension. He would always critique my sermon, mostly that it was too long. He was a realtor; when we were selling the house at 768 Gilpin, he was angry that we didn't use him; we had used Pat Mclheney, the mother of Barrie's friend.

When Bill was sick, I would visit him. He wasn't an unbeliever but never really opened his heart to the Lord. He was dying of cancer; during one visit, I exclaimed, "Bill, you are a damn fool! You are dying. The Lord is going to meet you, and you have to have an open heart to Him. Are you ready to open your heart fully?" And he said yes. So he prayed with me.

One day, out of the blue, I felt prompted to phone Carl Wells. I said, "Hi Carl. How are you doing? I'd like to meet with you." He told me, "I'm dying of cancer." That took me back, and I asked if I could come visit him. He was in hospice care, and I contacted his wife, Allie, to inquire about his condition. She affirmed that he had fast-moving cancer and would die in a rather short time. I had been his friend, and I would go with him to lunch sometimes, but I hadn't been in touch with him more recently. So when I called him, I was thinking of lunch, unaware that he was ill. When I went to see him, he shared that a hospice worker came to visit him, and when I asked what she advised, he answered, "She said to pray and laugh a lot."

In hindsight, I wish I had gone back to review our history. He had said to me during that difficult time at Ascension that the group who wanted me to leave had asked him, as my friend and influential church member, to meet with them. I told him I didn't want them to meet without my being there. So he told the group and didn't meet. I had always thought of myself as being approachable and I didn't care what they told me; I just wanted to be a better priest for them. But I wish I had reviewed all of that with Carl as he lay in bed. I wanted to know if he was offended by all any of that. He was a great reconciler himself, was well regarded in the Diocese, and had figured big in my life. I worried that I had interrupted what he felt called to do for the church. In hindsight, I would have told him, "You were so influential in my life and essential to my coming to Ascension. I should have let you meet with that group." But I didn't.

I brought him communion, and I went back to see him again. I wanted to be there when Allie came, and I brought them both communion. He actually looked pretty good on that visit. But then I had to go out of town, and when I returned his whole body had deteriorated in such a short time. Soon after, he died. The funeral was held at St. Christopher's, where Carl and Allie attended. The priest there was a really good guy and was a friend of Carl's.

Julie and Dave were a couple that used to be so critical of me at Ascension and came to me on Christmas Eve to tell me that they were leaving the church. Many years later, when he was very, very sick, he called me and told me he had cancer and asked me to pray with him. I never had trouble forgiving him, and it was a real privilege to pray with him and help him prepare to die.

When my brother Lee was dying, his whole family was around the bed at the hospital. The night before, we had celebrated the Eucharist in the room. It was Valentine's Day. Lee and Pat had separately picked the same card to give to each other. It was beautiful; his whole family was there. I stood at his side and recited a lot of scriptures.

I quoted Jeremiah 31:3: "I have loved you with an everlasting love; I have drawn you with loving kindness. I will build you up again."

He looked up at me and said, "Jim, I like that one." So the prayer became, "Draw me, draw me, Lord, draw me to yourself."

I wanted to speak at my brother's funeral, but the Catholic
Church didn't allow it. I read a prayer at my dad's funeral and sang at
my mother's. I didn't get to see Pat when she was dying. They had
lined everyone up to take turns being with her, and it wasn't my turn.
Billy was there, and he tried very hard to get Pat to get better and
stronger. But she died a very peaceful death. I don't know if anyone
was with her; I had wanted to be there. She and I had a very special
relationship; I had introduced her to the gospel of John when we were
in Berlin.

Regrets

One regret is from when my father was dying. Pat and Lee had gone back to Europe, and they wanted me to stay with him while they were gone. So I did, but I was anxious to get back home to Ascension and Barbara and the kids. He asked me to stay longer, and I didn't. I regret that. He wanted me to stay and reflect on his life with him. He grew up with alcoholic parents. His father would come home, and Dad would wrestle him to the floor to get the money so they could buy groceries.

I would send Dad messages. It was very important to me that he had the right idea about his belief in God. My dad had always prayed that God would make him a better man. But I believed it was all about Jesus. I sent him a banner that had a picture of a cat holding on for dear life, and the message was to hold onto and believe in Jesus, that He is our lifeline. I believe that the Lord wanted Dad to trust Him in his final moments.

But I didn't recognize that what Dad really wanted was to express his love for me and the family and to receive my love for him; he needed that in his dying. I've suffered over that when I think about it. When I went back a month later to be at his bedside, I said to him, "Dad, you are soon going to be with Mom." He flipped his head to the side, and that really got him; I think he didn't feel worthy of being in the same company as her. She was very religious, and she was the one who kept him going to church. The last night of his life, I slept on the floor at the foot of his bed with Billy (Lee's son) at his bedside. We woke up, knowing he was down the home stretch and he was getting ready to let go of this world. We ran to get Pat and Lee, and together we prayed many prayers. Billy was really good; he had a lot of faith. My heart ached for my dad as he left this world to go to Jesus. I deeply loved and admired him and what he had achieved in life.

Confronting Racism

When I was Coordinator of Personnel during my early Marianist career, I visited all of the high schools within the Marianist province in the central US (Kalamazoo, Pittsburgh, Cleveland, Cincinnati, Memphis), talking with and supporting the brothers and students, giving talks, leading retreats, and interviewing the brothers.

On one such trip, I went to Memphis. It was February, and the weather was springlike. I was asked to lead the retreat for a group of high school seniors. One of the lay teachers offered us his cabin at a lake. I showed them a documentary about Helen Keller. I asked the boys to pair off and lead one another blindfolded in the house and around the property to experience tactile sensitivity to the environment in the absence of sight. At the end of the morning, we decided to go swimming and took canoes across the lake to the beach. Among the students was a bright and handsome Black kid who, after graduation, had a commission to West Point.

At the beach, the kids started throwing footballs. There were a number of people on the beach. I was on a pier in the middle of the lake. When I looked up, I saw a posse of state police coming toward the kids. I dove off the pier and swam to the beach. I introduced myself to the policeman: "I'm a priest and here with these kids on a retreat. Are the boys bothering people with the football?" The state trooper abruptly said, "You got to get that nigger boy off the beach." I was stunned and upset. I asked him, "Officer, did you go to church this morning?" "Yes, now get that nigger boy off the beach." I asked, "Do you believe in Jesus? How can you make that assessment of this boy who is a very fine young man?" He answered, "We have a whole group of men in cars down that road, and if there is any trouble, they will come immediately." I saw that my appeal to his humanity and faith was going nowhere, so we got out of there quickly. I was hurt and deeply offended for my student's sake; that was my first experience of racial prejudice. I don't think I addressed it directly with the boys; I was so embarrassed. I knew the young man was going to be alright; he was going to West Point. When we got back to the cabin, we established our centeredness in God, as He was the light and leading each one of us. I just completely discounted that trooper in my mind and consciousness.

Many years later, in Denver, I went to Smiley's Dry Cleaning. There was a young African-American Air Force Cadet complaining that there was a hole in his sweater that hadn't been there when he brought it in. They hit the alarm calling for the police. I watched the whole event that ensued. The Denver policeman was really tough on the cadet. When he cuffed him and was taking him to the patrol car, the cadet broke into tears. I followed them out to the street and explained to the officer that I had watched the entire exchange and that the cadet wasn't being disrespectful. I was dressed as a priest. The officer said to me, "I don't give you advice on how to do your job in church." I said, "Well, you would be the only one." He said, "Let me see your license," so I gave it to him. I said, "Officer, can I see your badge?" I got his name and badge number and called the precinct when I returned home. I said I would like to make a report; I briefly told the story and wanted to know the whereabouts of the young cadet. I learned that the policeman was just getting off duty when he had arrived at Smiley's. The precinct told me that if the cadet was being detained, he would be taken to the main station, and it would take a day to find out if he was in there. My hope was that after our interaction, he simply drove the young man around the block.

One Christmas Eve, I had stopped into 7-11 to pick up a few items for the kids and encountered two young men, one white and one

African-American, arguing and measuring each other, getting ready for a fight. So I stepped in close to them and asked "Do you know that this is Christmas Eve? And the angels declared God's peace to the shepherds. God wants His peace to reach every person." By bringing Jesus into the middle of their standoff, it diffused the situation, and they moved on.

The Core of My Faith

The most underlying reality and truth in my life is the unconditional love of God for us.

Where does that come from? It comes from the reality of Jesus Himself.

John 3:16: "God so loved the world that He gave His only Son so that everyone who believes in Him will not be lost but have eternal life."

Hebrews 1:1-3 inspires me: "In the past, God spoke to our forefathers through the prophets at many times and in various ways, but in the last days, He has spoken to us by His Son, whom He appointed heir of all things and through whom He made the universe. The Son is the radiance of God's glory and the exact representation of His being, sustaining all things by His powerful word."

The preeminence of Jesus: "No one comes to the Father except through me." Jesus said the sin of the world was that "they didn't believe in Me." The sin of the Pharisees was to deliberately deny the truth of who Jesus is. He said to them, "You will die in your sin because you did not believe in me." It is the deliberate decision against believing in Him. The works He performed were to show that He was acting in the power of God.

As a junior in high school, I started to read the Gospel of John. The prelude to that Gospel is, "In the beginning was the Word, and the Word was with God, and the Word was God ...."

The first reality in my worldview is that Jesus is Lord, and God, and Savior. No one comes to the Father except through Him.

Many will ask, "'What about those who don't hear about Jesus?'" Jesus is the way to the Father but I also believe that God sees the heart of a person. He is looking for love. God is love.

The God I began to know, and the Jesus I began to know, was an intimate God, meaning He was in the heart and soul of us. God within.

That was the first reality in my mind and heart as a teenager: that God wasn't high in the sky, but in my very soul. Jesus said, "On that day you will know that I am in you, and you are in Me." I love that promise!!

Who is Jesus? Phillip said, "Show us the Father, and that will be enough for us." At the Last Supper, Jesus asked, "Have I been so long with you, and you do not know me? The person who sees me, sees the Father." Jesus, in His human nature, is the perfect copy of the Father.

Once this was established in my soul and my mind, I really fed on it. This is what changed in me. From a very young age, in my journey with Jesus, I was always trying to see myself as worthy. This characterized me most as a teenager. I was always trying to measure up. And I kept feeding that with, "I'm not number one" because my dad said at my birth, "by all means, save my wife." This was repeated many times growing up and therefore really embedded in me. I knew my dad had wanted me to live, but I believed I was not the first choice. I was important, but not of first importance. This perception carried throughout my life. The person I was working with or trying to help was always more important than me. If dessert was dished out, the others should have it first. My existence was only to be a help or service to others. My preferences were not first. This drove me in everything

I did; always trying to measure up to what I thought others expected of me.

As an example, I would go to great pains to do things for my mother. She said, "you are the only one that helps me when I ask." I took pride in that, being the one to help her.

It wasn't very hard for me to be self-effacing. When I approached the Novice Master, Fr. Martin, about my feelings of inferiority, he said to me, "You don't have an inferiority complex, you are just inferior." It was kind of a joke, but it also resonated with me. I always felt myself unworthy, so I would try to measure up to God. I would try to keep that image of how I was acting or thinking, helping or not helping others. That was at the top of my daily checklist – was I there for others?

It became an important self-assessment. When I failed, was selfish, self-centered, or sinful, it would take a big toll on me. I would work hard to get back into the light, to the image of myself that I imagined God saw me in. I would work hard to make up for it. I became very scrupulous as a teenager and young adult.

Working against that was the truth that God loves me no matter what. It's not how good I am but how good God is. Because He is good and He loves me exactly the way I am.

But meanwhile, if I fell short of the mark, I not only felt guilty but also sort of crushed. God was out to heal that. It was a question of time to change, but it took a lot of years. One of the big influences in this was Brennan Manning and his book Abba Father. What he set out to prove is that he was among the worst of the sinners, sharing that he committed fornication, adultery, shamefully talked about other people, and so on. But what Brennan came to realize, and what I eventually came to realize, is that God loves us not because we have earned His love, but because of who He is. He is a God who loves every person unconditionally. It landed in my soul that God loves me in spite of myself or any merit on my part.

For many years I had tried to hold onto God; to grab hold of His shirttail, like a child learning to skate. I was holding on for dear life and worked very hard at it. But the change that came about, in more recent years, is that I don't have to hold on to God because He holds onto me. That realization absolutely changed my life. He loves unconditionally, I'm immersed in Him, and He is just going to bring me through. With a new awareness of who He is, a new day is arriving.

I operate with the belief that something in each person mirrors some measure of God's likeness, and I look for that in each one. I know that God wants to dwell fully in the heart of every person and I want that too.

The other big highlight in my worldview was to learn to throw myself completely upon the love, and goodness, and power of God in my life: the virtue of trust and attitude in my mind, heart, and soul. Later in my time at Ascension, when I made the 30-day retreat at Sacred Heart Retreat House, I wrote to each of my kids; the main message was to trust in the Lord.

A lot of reassurance came from reading Brennan Manning. He was so trusting in his love of God that it didn't matter what people thought of him. Gradually, I got to the point that it didn't matter what

people thought of me. My image of myself, my persona, didn't matter. I should just know that Godloved me as I am. Brennan Manning said God not only loves you, He likes you. God sees throughall of our faults and past defects. It was a real change in mindset, but more than that, a change insoul.

The driving forces in my life are:

➢ A God within.

➢ A God whom I can trust.

➤ A God who loves me just as I am.

I believe that and rest my case on that belief. But I have also come to feel this in my innermost soul. Do I always feel it? No. But I keep believing and recommitting to that belief in God and His promises to us. Then comes the immediate transfer of that belief to any person I encounter —- that at their innermost person, they are valued and loved by God.

Parenting

The birth of the kids, their starting to walk, going to school, starting sports, and going to college—these were all landmarks in our lives.

James Aaron

Jeffrey Michael

Ryan Kern

Barrie Elizabeth

Robyn Sage

All of our kids were born in Connecticut except Robyn; she was born at Rose Hospital in Denver.

Every birth was a great joy, and every child had a reason for being illustrious.

Jay was the first. He was a strong baby. My brother Lee came when he was born and extended his two forefingers to pick him up, noting how he held onto Lee's fingers as he lifted him. Jeff was the second child and was very adorable. He was a very even-tempered child. Ryan, number three, was an easy baby and maintained that ease as an infant and growing up. His was the only birth I missed. I had gone down to get coffee as it was late, and I wanted to stay awake. By the time I got back to the birthing room, he had already arrived!

When Barrie came along, she was a wonderful surprise, the first girl after three boys!

Later on, she was featured on the cover of Baby Talk maga-zine. When we went home to Mt. Lebanon to see my family, my brother Lee commented on how beautiful she was and said she could be a model. Last but certainly not least came Robyn. She decided she wasn't going to come in the normal time frame; she needed an extra two weeks. True to form, she came on her own terms. For two weeks, our friends Carolyn and Mike Spence were on call, expecting to come and stay with the kids, but it didn't happen. When she was finally born, we were debating whether to name her Robyn or Kacie. I said, "Hi Kacie," and she burst into tears; then I said, "Robyn," and she im-mediately quieted down. When the kids arrived later in the afternoon, Barrie came into the room announcing, "My baby sister Wobyn." That sealed the deal.

Jay, at an early age, was very good at doors and locks; the kids would come to visit me at church, and he could operate and unlock the doors. We thought he was so smart. No child is as smart as your first child. But each child was smart in his or her own right.

Jay and Jeff both started into Montessori in preschool. Jeff al-ways did everything right at school; when the teacher left the room and the kids were out of line, he would stand up and take charge of the class.

Ryan was a good child and the one that every teacher really liked. They would say if we could just clone him. As a little boy, he would hear the children's books we read at night and memorize them. So when he started preschool at Montview Presbyterian Church, he looked like a whiz,; he was reciting, but they thought he was reading the book.

Barrie was the perfect child in school and would befriend kids who were immigrants or children of immigrants. She would conduct individual children around the grocery store, teaching them English by naming the products while shopping. The teachers really liked her –

she was very dependable and would step up to take charge of the situation. Barrie liked to go to King Soopers to ask for a 'homemade' cookie.

Robyn started Sunday school, and Nancy Downing was teaching. She was a very nice lady and taught Sunday school for many years. Robyn was usually late because the family was late getting to church, and when she walked in, Nancy would say, "Good morning, Robyn." Robyn would come home and imitate her. Robyn hated to be singled out.

None of the kids were exactly shy. Jay would play guitar and sing. At Wyman, he had a lead part in the HMS Pinafore and sang a solo. At Dora Moore Elementary School, he sang and played guitar to "The Gambler." He was very bright but did not like being in school and having the teacher tell him what to do. Jay attended Morey Middle School, and it was not a great experience for him academically. So we looked for opportunities to send the rest of the kids to private school for the middle school years.

Ryan and Jeff went to Kent Middle School on an inner-city scholarship. They could have continued at Kent for high school. Ryan, following Jeff and Jay's lead, was a good athlete; he played football, basketball, and lacrosse. But both boys wanted to go to Denver East High School; Ryan called it "the real world."

Robyn started kindergarten at Dora Moore, where all of the kids had attended, in a bilingual class. She did well; I don't know if she learned a whole lot, but she learned to speak Spanish. We soon realized that Robyn needed to be challenged academically, so it was a good move when we were able to get both Barrie and Robyn into St. Anne's Episcopal School. That was a great experience for both of them. Both of the girls received scholarships and financial aid; Rose was the employee at the school who monitored the scholarships and got a great package for the girls.

Jeff was head boy at East High School in his senior year, and then Ryan followed suit.

All the kids were very friendly, had lots of friends, and were often out with friends.

Every child is an individual and has their own values, preferences, and skills. I realized that I needed to consider them and their choices individually. The challenge I found in parenting is how to help them realize that they are loved completely but differently. That is usually interpreted by the child by how they are treated. If one child gets away with more or is punished less, then they are the ones who are loved more. When Jay was a senior in high school, he had an 11:00 p.m. curfew. I would wait up for him on a Saturday night, and if he was even 10 minutes late, I would be very upset with him. But when Barrie was in high school, she didn't have a curfew and would come home quite late. Jay would say to me, "Dad, Barrie can stay out until any hour, and you don't get upset." How does a child interpret that they are loved and trusted?

Physical hugging and acts of kindness are how a child can see themselves as really loved. It doesn't mean giving the child everything they want. The children would often say, "That's not fair, Mom," and Barb would reply, "Fair is a carnival that comes in the spring." When each child is born, whether 1, 3, or 5, they are loved completely, and the parent is thrilled at the birth of that child. For the older siblings, they are so excited about the birth of the baby and become protective of their younger siblings. The older children fill in the gap during the growth of their siblings and are of assistance to the parents.

I can picture the boys holding their sisters when they were born, and they knew they had a job to do. As they got older, they had to protect their sisters when they were crossing the street—they had to take their hands.

As a husband and a father, I felt like I became wiser and more practical when working with couples preparing for marriage. With the experience of being married and having a family, I could really tune into subjects that they needed to discuss. In marriage counseling, I used FOCUS. The important subject matter always came out through this assessment.

In premarital counseling, I was able to draw on my own experiences and examples. I was more astute and insightful because of it. I'd say about 75% of the couples were already in a marriage-like relationship when they showed up for counseling. I don't think that was necessarily unhealthy.

After my many years of marriage and premarital counseling, my advice for my own children and grandchildren is to love your spouse and be very open to listening. Prepare your mind ahead of time to not react quickly in discussions or arguments. That's been a challenge for me with Barbara: to not react right away. And give your spouse hugs after you've been battling.

In both marriage and parenting, I learned to try to pose my perspective as a question. Do you think it's possible to do that a little differently? Have you ever considered...? Or simply state, "Tell me what your plan is." As the parent, you have to figure out a way to work with your kids. Ask questions for clarity. For example, when Robyn was in college, she called me to tell me that she wanted to go to Spain for her semester break. I simply replied, "Tell me about it, honey. What is your plan?" As we spoke, I decided that she had considered all of the angles and that it would work for her to go. I said okay, and she seemed surprised. "Really, Dad?!"

A collection of photos of our family over the years

The Wilsons

My time with the Wilsons, Jen's family, was a very important time for me. Jay and Jen had met at Gettysburg College and eventually married. I really liked the Wilsons and spent a lot of time and really dedicated myself to Jen's parents, Rich and Pat. Every time we went to East Hampton, certainly at Jay and Jen's wedding and her brother George's and Danielle's wedding, we would visit with the Wilsons. Jay and Jen had a beautiful wedding, and a lot of our extended family attended. Rich read the prayers of the people, and I co-celebrated with the Catholic priest at the ceremony.

I had also counseled Jen's cousin, Ann, and her fiancé before they were married. Then, after they were married and having trouble, they came to Virginia Beach for a three-day counseling retreat, and it was very powerful. They really came back together. I had the 500 Club pray for them. Those situations of prayer support are so important for a couple. They came to the realization that they wanted to stay together, and they are still together now.

Over the years, we would visit with Rich and Pat a lot back and forth, even after Jay and Jen divorced. I remember sitting with Barb in their home, and they both told me that neither one of them had any real belief in the Lord, and it greatly saddened me. They were a great couple, and I believed it would be only time until their faith in Jesus was activated. When we visited, we would attend St. Luke's Church with them. We always tried to capitalize on that time, expressing our faith and discussing the scriptures we had heard. George and Danielle would also come regularly to the Sunday Eucharist. Barbara and I tried to uplift and encourage them; I would also talk with the priest about them. He was also a former Catholic clergyman, so we had a similar background.

I used to walk a lot with Rich, and he talked to me about himself and his life. Some of it was positive, and some of it was not; he struggled with depression. On one of our walks, he shared with me that one morning he was out walking, looked at the sky, and had a theophany experience. The beauty of the morning light really impacted him and gave him a sense of the awesomeness of God. I reminded him of that experience later on when he was struggling. When he was in the hospital for his depression, I would go and visit him in an effort to encourage him and pray with him. At times, I would invite some of the family to come and join in prayer for Rich.

Years later, when he was dying, I was frequently on the phone with Jen and Pat. But I never got to speak with Rich directly before he died. Rich had a great heart; he was a good father and husband. I really grieved his dying and his questions around his faith.

Singapore

In 1987, I met Fr. Dave Stitt at a charismatic conference. Fr. Dave was an American missionary at an Anglican church in Singapore. We invited each other to do a church exchange. This sounded like a perfect family fun time with Barbara and all the kids.

The day of our departure, flying out of Denver to San Francisco, the agent from United called and said the departure time was moved up. She said that would give us an hour to get ready and out the door. I told her we didn't leave early. She said, "Well, if you want to go today, you have to leave an hour early." Everyone was awakened to get going. Our friend, Jane Kindall had offered to come and straighten the house after we left to prepare it for the Stitts; it was a disaster as we had left in such a fury. We arrived at the airport, confirmed the gate, and then ran down the concourse—all seven of us, each with one carry-on bag. Most important among the possessions was the KLM bag, carrying Barbara's 'snake oil' and other remedies and medication for any ailment we may encounter in our two months in Southeast Asia. Very quickly, the kids tagged her as the 'drug queen.' Anytime we went anywhere, the question was, "Who has the KLM bag?"

We connected in San Francisco to Singapore and arrived at the beautiful and modern airport in Singapore. Jay noticed the banner across the wall: "Drug possession is punishable by death." At 16, that really impressed him. We heard later that if you stole anything, they would chop off your hand or fingers. Otherwise, the arrival seemed promising.

Singapore was noted for its warm hospitality. The first evening, we were invited to the home of an East Indian Singaporean family. The aroma permeated the house, and we were all introduced to curry seasoning. The family was most welcoming. That was a pleasant beginning compared to the next morning when Dave and Dee Stitt invited us to visit the wet market, which, in case you don't know (we didn't), was all the hanging evidence of slaughtered animals. It was a cultural shock and part of our orientation to living in Southeast Asia. The evening of the first full day, we were again invited to dinner at the home of the Soh family. The children spent that night enjoying a sleepover. The Loh and Soh families became some of our closest friends during that seven-week stay.

The boys with the Soh and Loh children in Singapore

So much happened during that time in Singapore. I gave sermons at St. Helen's. Dave was inspired by my account of the prayer marches I had helped to lead in Denver during a time of violence and decided he would like to stage a march through the neighborhood as a demonstration of the Christian faith. It was a very evangelical

Anglican church. One of the first Sundays, an outdoor baptism for over 20 adult candidates took place.

Singapore was so hot. Halfway through the service, the priest needed to go to the sacristy and change albs (the priest's robe). After a couple of weeks, we traveled by train and bus on the peninsula to the beautiful highlands of Malaysia, where the British officers would go for R&R for a church retreat. On the train, I met a middle-aged man who was an administrator at a hospital in Malaysia. During our conversation, he shared that he was a Buddhist, and I shared that we were Christian. We proceeded to share our beliefs. I told him about my belief in Jesus Christ, and it seemed that he was absorbing some of the revelation about the Lord. As we were getting ready to depart the train, I told him that I hoped someday he would come to know the Lord.

Arriving at the Malaysian resort, we were surprised by the luxury. We were told we were going to a church camp, and we were expecting something along the lines of Trinity Ranch (our church camp in the mountains of Colorado). Instead- we encountered a five star resort. Someone had commented that Singaporeans went camping first class; in today's vernacular, it would be called glamping.

We ate breakfast in the clouds; it was a huge dining room with windows open, and the clouds would move through in the morning. The room accommodations were beautiful. The large swimming pool was exciting for the kids. We had a baptism there. It was an incredible week.

At the end of the week, there was a talent show. The kids, Barbara, and I performed a lip sync to Billy Joel's "For the Longest Time." But we were upside down and covering our faces with sunglasses on our chins. The crowd was in hysterics.

Special events included golf, which involved crossing fairways where other golfers were playing. We had to be careful, to say the least.

There was a woman greenskeeper; she would sweep the greens and clear any debris. Hiking in the surrounding woods, we noticed ant trails and were told not to interrupt the march of the ants. It was an impressive trail. Jeff was the videographer and narrator at different times during our stay there.

One night, we were at a restaurant dining at a table outside. We heard what sounded like a tiny helicopter moving in, and a giant rhinoceros beetle landed in the middle of our table. Startled, all seven of us exclaimed and jumped up. The waitress saw the commotion and came over, picked up the beetle, and threw it over the balcony.

After the retreat, we traveled around Southeast Asia, in Malaysia, Thailand, and Hong Kong. We took a bus down through the highlands to Kuala Lumpur. Surprisingly, the bus stopped in the middle of the night at a huge outdoor market, featuring all kinds of exotic foods. Passengers boarded the bus with live chickens, televisions, and all sorts of purchased items. Being an American family of seven, we were the oddity among the passengers. We then traveled to Penang to a beach resort and had many adventures. We took an excursion in the South China Sea in a low-sitting boat with an outboard engine. I asked the guy, "What are those eels in the water?" He said they were electric eels and their bite could be deadly. We had taken the boat to an island and came upon the largest jellyfish we had ever seen washed up on the beach. It had to be two to three feet in diameter. The boys found a thick stick and tried to flip it over, but it broke the stick. We rented jet skis, and the kids had fun driving through the water filled with jellyfish. The kids went parasailing. Jay and Jeff had successful flights. Robyn wasn't heavy enough, so the guide hung freely on the ropes behind her to weigh her down a bit. Ryan also wasn't quite heavy enough but had flown alone and taken Barrie's camera to capture photos. He was going down into the water, and the last thing you saw was his hand holding up the camera. Thankfully, he was fine, but the camera never quite recovered. After viewing all of this, Barrie opted out of parasailing. The South China Sea was tropical and filled with many dangerous creatures.

Barbara was stung by a jellyfish at the beach; it was incredibly painful. She said it was worse than the birth of our five children. I was also having trouble with my knee and signed up for acupuncture. But I got an infection, and my leg became swollen, making it difficult to walk. Luckily, we had the KLM bag for all of our ailments.

We then traveled to Bangkok by plane. Robyn was so insistent that she be allowed to carry her own passport, so she did and promptly left it on the plane. The boys teased her that she was going to have to stay and live in Thailand, and she was terribly frightened. Airport personnel drove out to the plane on the runway to retrieve her passport.

In Bangkok we visited an orphanage. The children in the orphanage all wanted our boys to pick them up, especially Jay because he was so tall. They would say "Papa Un," when asking to be held. There was a little girl who was drawn to us, and we were drawn to her; we thought maybe we should adopt her. We contacted an agency to inquire, but we didn't qualify. In hindsight, we realized that the Lord knew this wasn't the right fit.

We flew from Bangkok to Hong Kong. We had been asked to help carry bibles and Christian material into China, so when we were in Hong Kong, we took a special training on how to carry materials into China. Jay said, "Oh boy, we are learning how to smuggle!" From Hong Kong, we took a train to cross into China. When we arrived at the station, there were guards everywhere and a watchtower. There were signs posted to not take photos, but I felt compelled to take a few, and the guard saw me and waved his fingers in reprimand. Meanwhile, we were all loaded down with pamphlets, books, and bibles. We had a large commentary, and we decided the best idea was to put it in Robyn's bag with her stuffed panda bear sticking out. We were advised that I shouldn't carry anything because, as an adult, if I were caught, the punishment for me would be more severe. We met two women in a restaurant and handed over all the materials under the table. We purchased bowls and spoons and then returned to Hong Kong.

The thing I remember most about Hong Kong is that we went to a water park. We had taken a bus but gotten off too soon, and so we walked a long way to the park. This is where the kids learned that I couldn't slide on a water slide. For some reason, I always got stuck. The kids thought it was hilarious.

We flew from Hong Kong to Seattle much heavier than when we departed, with many acquired purchases, including a new stereo Jay purchased in Hong Kong.

When we landed in Denver after being gone for seven weeks, I informed the kids that we weren't going home but continuing on to a charismatic conference in New Orleans. Jay was upset, to say the least, and threatened to stowaway. A parishioner met us at the airport to collect our unnecessary baggage and purchases, and we continued on to New Orleans.

We stayed at a condo in the French Quarter, and the conference was held at the Superdome. They had buses that would transport people back and forth to the conference. One day at the conference, Barbara, Barrie, Robyn, and I were sitting on a lower level, and the boys had gone to sit higher up. Barrie wanted to join them and went to find them. Meanwhile, they had left. She then came down to find us, but we also departed, believing she was with the boys, leaving her stranded in the Superdome at 10 years old. This was Barrie's first encounter of being on her own in an unfamiliar city. She drew on her own ingenuity and found the correct bus to make her own way back to the French Quarter, found the condo, and came up to the second floor to the room where Barbara and I were. She knocked at the door, and I remember saying, "Hi, Barrie," and she burst into tears. We didn't even know she was missing, as we believed her to be with the boys.

When we came back from the summer away, Carl Wells handed me a letter that Dave Stitt had written, making his pitch to become the priest of Ascension. After I read it, Carl ripped the letter up and threw it in the trash. Dave came from a business background, and I think he was used to going after what he wanted. I saw him some time later at a Diocesan Convention, and he said to me, "Now don't attack me for that letter." I told him I would never attack him. They ended up at a parish in Iowa, and we didn't hear from them after that.

Medjugorje

Starting in the early 1980s, Mary appeared in visions to six young people in a small village in Bosnia-Hercegovina named Medjugorje. A woman at Ascension gave me a tape about the visions, and I immediately knew it was the real thing. I was struck by the reactions of the village and the growing interest and devotion to the Blessed Mother.

St. James Church in Medjugorje

We made three pilgrimages in four years. Those trips were timely in a spiritual way, but also in the fact that we could physically get there before the war. Medjugorje had a big impact on my formation. The first year a group went, including Bill and Peg

Humphrey. That year, a woman was supposed to go but couldn't, so she gave her ticket and reservations to Barbara. The second trip was with Pat and Bill Copeland and Nancy and Dennis Callaghan. They were all very good friends and shared this incredible experience with us. The third trip was when we took our kids.

Our pilgrimage to Medjugorje with Pat and Bill Copeland

The only visionaries I got to know a bit were Marija and Vicka. We stayed at Marija's brother's home. Everyone was so nice.

There was a priest who was their spiritual director, and he took a real interest in the kids. I asked him if I could go into the choir loft when Marija had a vision of Mary in the early evening. I was in the balcony with a few other people when Marija was experiencing a vision, and when she turned around and looked at me with such powerful love, it went right to my soul. I was so certain of Mary's presence in the room. I asked Marija after she returned from a retreat, what was something she took from the experience. She answered, "Give yourself completely to God and put your whole trust in Him." Barb elbowed me and said, "That is for you."

On our second trip, after a service we went out and saw the miracle of the sun. We stared at the sun, and the disc moved over it, and the colors shot out from behind it. Barbara and I still have this gift today and sit on the bench at the park in Lowry and gaze at the afternoon sun. And the experience of fulminating flowing colors still occurs. It is a gift that has never ceased and is a constant reminder that Mary is still looking after us and our family.

With Maria at her home in Medjugorje

Chile

After finishing college, Barrie worked at a family resort, The Gran Hotel Pucon, in Pucon, Chile, with two of her girlfriends. Barbara and I made a last-minute decision to visit her. Miraculously, we got the final flight out of Denver to Miami on Super Bowl weekend, which Miami was hosting. We flew from Denver to Miami to Santiago and arrived in the morning. We then caught a flight to Temuco and took a Volkswagen bus to Pucon. After 18+ hours of travel, we were within a mile and a half of the resort when our car was rear-ended. It was a significant impact, and our seat was dislodged, but thankfully we weren't hurt. There was a dispute over the cause of the accident, and we went to bat for our driver legally, as he was not at fault. Ultimately, we arrived at the resort and were checked in at the front desk by Anne Brueck, Barrie's college roommate and one of the triumvirate.

Barrie came in quickly from her activities and helped to get us settled into the room. She then invited us to the dining room for a luxurious, white linen dinner. There were many families with children. We enjoyed the VIP treatment with Barrie, who was a GO (one of the sports and animation staff) and responsible for hosting and entertaining the guests.

The girls had stayed as guests at the hotel before they were hired. One of the team saw Barrie dancing in the bar and invited her to audition to be on the sports and animation team; they put on a show every night but Sunday with dancing and sketches. After dinner, we went to see the show; it was a lot of fun. Barrie and the other performers practiced every afternoon for the evening show, and the performers looked very well prepared. The show lasted until midnight, and I found it extraordinary that the families with small children would stay up for the entire show.

The next morning, we slept in and then enjoyed the activities of the resort. Barrie was back on the job, leading an aerobics class and giving clear instructions in Spanish. We sat in the back of the room and were amazed at her expertise. We had a very nice day and enjoyed the activities of the resort. Meanwhile, we were anticipating the Super Bowl.

Barrie had reserved a table at a restaurant for us to watch the game. Denver was playing against the Atlanta Falcons. Barrie's friends Anne and Rachael, along with a few of their local friends, joined us. Rachael was working as a tour guide at an Eco-Tourism shop; she led hikes throughout the Lake Region. We were a strong cheering section for the Broncos, and there was one other American family there cheering for the Falcons. It was a struggle to keep the restaurant focused on the game instead of a local futbol (soccer) match. It was a close game. At one point, the Broncos were gaining ground and about to score when the local Chilean network interrupted for a commercial break. Clearly, American football didn't receive the same regard as futbol. Nevertheless, we had a great time, saw most of the game, and the Broncos won!

In the following days, we enjoyed visiting with the girls, went window shopping, and relaxed at the black sand beach with the sleeping volcano looming behind us. It was the peak of the summer, and the beach was very crowded. One afternoon we visited the hot spring with Anne and Rachael while Barrie was working. We also enjoyed observing /participating in the activities Barrie led: bingo, water aerobics, beach volleyball, and Latin dance lessons on the veranda. And, of course, we enjoyed dinner and the show every night.

It was hard saying goodbye at the end of the week. Flying back to Denver through Miami was easy and uneventful, and we felt so blessed that we were able to have been in Chile with Barrie and her friends.

Guantanamo Bay

In 2005 Amy was serving as a Navy doctor and was assigned to Guantanamo Bay. She was the only OB/GYN for the three military branches there. They had the three older boys at the time. Barbara and I went to visit Jeff, Amy and the boys during their assignment. They stayed in a very nice home in the officers' quarters. The view from their backyard overlooked the Guantanamo Bay detention camp; we could look out and see the prisoners in their orange jumpsuits. We could also look out over the hills and see where Castro staged his revolution. There were iguanas running all over the place, like you would see squirrels here. We really enjoyed our visit; we went to the beach to swim in the bay and to the pool. We couldn't leave the base, but it had everything we needed. One of the guards from the prison came to the pool, and I asked him what it was like guarding the prisoners. He said it was rough; the prisoners would call them names, spit at them, and so forth.

China

Believe it or not, in 2008 we went back to China. What a surprise when Jeff and his wife Amy invited us to travel with them to China to pick up the two little girls they had adopted. We flew out of San Francisco with them and their three boys on South China Airline to Beijing. It seemed we were the only Americans on the flight. Night flights are always hard; we watched movies in Chinese with English subtitles. Dinner was served: a meat, vegetable, and rice dinner. And they served what seemed to be the same meal in the morning.

We arrived in Beijing just one month after the Summer 2008 Olympics. The drive in from the airport was tree-lined, and I was told they had planted $2 billion in shrubbery in preparation for the Olympics. It was so beautiful and very lush with trees, plants, flowers, and shrubs.

We stayed in a nice four-star hotel in Beijing and spent a couple of days in orientation. The first day was a tour of the city. I was amazed by how Western it felt, with the music and the Olympic displays still on display. When we arrived in the city and departed the bus, Noah, at two years old, shouted "Ni Hao" (hello in Mandarin).

Wherever we walked during our time in China, this American family with three blond-haired, blue-eyed boys drew attention. The starkest aspect of our presence was the fact that one family had three boys; this ran counter to the Chinese one-child policy. People continually, but politely, stopped us to take pictures of or with the children. Christian, at five years old, in particular, was sought out for photos, and at one point, he was so tired of posing that he announced very clearly, "Just one more picture!"

We went to Tiananmen Square, the site of the deadly protests. There we encountered more Americans and other international tourists. The Square really impressed me; it is rather striking and has a magnificent monument to ancient emperors. We took many photos as we meandered around the vast courtyard.

With Amy and Jeff (right) in Tiananmen Square

We were told we could climb the Great Wall, so we went by bus to the foot of the Great Wall and started to make our way up. It was quite the hike. Young men asked if they could carry Noah. It was very touristy; you could buy food and many other items at the base of the wall. It was the week of the Paralympics, and the afterglow of the Olympics was still strongly felt. The introductory climb was mild compared to the long steep ascent up the path on top of the wall. I remember there was a paraplegic man who was carried up the steps. We enjoyed the very strenuous but enjoyable ascent through the different landing places along the wall. It was absolutely beautiful.

That night, we enjoyed a delicious, first-class dinner at the hotel and were happy to return to our rooms to rest.

The second day, we caught a plane to Guangzhou. When we arrived at the British White Swan Hotel, it was like the lap of luxury; the fixtures in the bathroom were gold, the accommodations were perfect, and the staff and service were white-gloved. They had so many beautiful shops in the lobby. It was surprising how rich it all was.

We went to a meeting place in a big hall at the hotel where all the children to be adopted were brought. We were in high anticipation of the girls' arrival. Jeff and Amy had named the girls Mia and Sophia. They were not yet three, and they were so little.

We were then taken to a small room, and the orphanage administrators, an attractive young couple, came in with Mia and Sophia. The couple left abruptly without saying goodbye to the girls. Once the girls realized this, they began to wail. It was a very sad separation for them.

The next morning, we went out to the pool, which was wonderful. The boys had a great time swimming and we led the girls by the hand out to the water. We found a Chinese laundry down the street to clean our clothes. Someone suggested a bilingual church, which we attended, and when they burst out in song in English, chills ran up my spine. It was a spiritual highlight for me. It was an evangelistic church with a congregation made up of people mostly in their twenties, and the sermon was in English and Chinese. We were told you could get up in a public space and profess your faith, but we also learned that there were spies and everything was observed; however, we didn't have a sense of any danger for ourselves or the Chinese worshippers.

We had to go out for dinner; we preferred a few of the Italian restaurants, and the food was always very good.

One day, we went to a spectacular amusement park called White Cloud because it was up on a hill, above the smog of the city. They had all sorts of bird and animal shows. I saw a group of middle school children in their uniforms, and as they approached, I yelled, "Hip, hip hooray." They all got in on it and yelled back. The teacher was aghast, but it was so much fun. The children introduced themselves and inquired about us.

The hotel offered daily excursions, so every day we went out in the vans to another destination. We spent about three weeks enjoying China and getting acquainted with Mia and Sophia before we all returned home together.

Reconciliation

A lot of my life was a passing parade of people. There are too many people to name who have influenced me and shown me love and encouraged me. Even the people who have opposed me, I have not had the inclination to oppose them but rather to accept them and draw them in.

When Jesus appeared to the apostles after his resurrection, He said "My peace I give to you." How do we experience that peace? How is it transferred from Him to us?   Typically, if we devote our life to Jesus, He will establish His peace in our hearts. He declared "Blessed are the peacemakers, for they shall be called the children of God." Matthew 5:9

If we live close to Jesus we will have peace in spite of all the trials and tribulations in our life. We can always find that place where He dwells with us and within us, and call on Him to calm the troubled waters of our heart and soul.

The apostles very likely felt ashamed. His first word to them was "Shalom", the Jewish greeting of welcoming and forgiveness. Afterall, Peter had denied that he knew Jesus and the others abandoned Him in His great hour of suffering and need. But He didn't berate them. The only apostle he did berate was Thomas, who was absent at the moment of Jesus' first appearance. When the others told Thomas about seeing Jesus he declared "Unless I see the nail marks in His hands and put my finger where the nails were, and put my hand into His side, I will not believe." (John 20:25) Yet upon seeing Jesus Thomas exclaimed "My Lord and my God."

Jesus showed Thomas and the apostles his gracefulness and I try to emulate that grace with others, including those who have hurt or offended me. It makes me think of the familiar song, which I've added my own twist to:

Let there be peace on earth, let it begin with me. With God our Father and Christ our brother, brothers and sisters all are we, let me walk with my family in perfect harmony.

Jesus said that the greatest commandment is this: "As the Father has loved me, so do I love you. As I have loved you, so must you love one another. This is all I command you: Love one another." There is a transfer from God to Jesus, Jesus to us, and He urges us to pass it on.

In Matthew 5:43 Jesus says: "You have heard it was said Love your neighbor and hate your enemies. But I tell you: love your enemies and pray for those who persecute you, that you may be children of your Father in heaven."

For me, loving people who are disagreeable to me or for whom I am disagreeable to them, is my way of practicing this love for others even though that person may not appeal to me. Welcoming each person into the home of my heart is how I try to practice this way of being in potential relationship with each person. What do I find is the easiest way of practicing this welcoming of others? Simply by smiling and greeting them. People know if we are sincere and if we have a heart that receives them as God does.

Recently a young doctor at St. Lukes approached me and said, "I want to tell you that your smile rejuvenates me."

I am sure God wants us to welcome others and receive them. How can I practice this welcoming if I don't forgive the person who offends me? Forgiveness is a choice on our part. I may not have any emotion of forgiveness, but if I can decide to forgive that individual and be sincerely gracious to him or her then eventually the feeling of forgiveness will flow through my heart.

It is so important that we are willing to step out in faith to use the peace of the Lord for the reconciliation of ourselves and other people. So often in my conversations, I would get on to the topic of forgiveness. In marriage counseling, I often talked about the importance of continuing to forgive each other to couples. At Jeff's wedding, I felt led to talk about the importance of forgiveness. That so influenced my brother Lee that he sought out our nephew, Larry Aber, to talk to him, to seek forgiveness, and from there they built a relationship.

Lee and I at my son's wedding

Recently, I felt discouraged that I don't have as many opportunities now to welcome and encourage others. However, Ryan pointed out the many occasions that I have recently interacted and prayed with our neighbors, including one who is Jewish and as a teenager lived on a Kibbutz. She has been struggling with the war in Israel and anti-Jewish sentiments. As long as we are on this earth, God can use us for His purposes.

It's amazing to me how God uses every situation, for those tuned into Him, to bring people to an acknowledgement of what is important in their life and what needs to be done.

My worldview is totally involved with Jesus. The Resurrection is in the stuff of life. I die all the day long, but behold, I live so that the person of Jesus will become more evident in this weak flesh of mine. Jesus said "I am the resurrection and the life, the person who believes in me will live forever." Paul wrote that God is in Christ reconciling the world to Himself. "You are ambassadors of Christ, be reconciled." As followers of Christ, this is our mission as we move through the world.

Empowerment of the Holy Spirit

I thrill to the realization of Christ glorified. St. Paul says: "Christ in you, your hope of glory."

I really live through the power of the Holy Spirit. Like Jesus says in the Gospel, "not by bread alone does man live but by every word from the mouth of God." The word of God became very important to me.

This is what really turns on my soul: The thought of Jesus glorified, and my participation in that through faith and eventually through sight. That's my anticipation.

What has become essential in my walk is the truth and reality of God in how He works in the world and works in me.

Fr. Basel, a Trappist monk, was a great influence on how I pray. He traveled throughout the world to talk about centering prayer and getting people involved. Centering prayer is a way of practicing abandonment to God – which really thrills me. Anything in this life doesn't matter because I'm in His hands. Everything matters because of that, but the reality of the moment is that God is with me and with us, and He makes the difference that He wants to make.

Centering prayer is a person consciously sitting in the presence of God, having read something from Scripture and then basking in that word of God. When I'm practicing centering prayer and my mind begins to drift, I go back to one word— God, Jesus, Love, Hope, Joy— one word that will bring me back to my soul centered on God. It is a very important kind of prayer. This way of praying, like praying in the name of Jesus, is very powerful. When I would get a negative thought or a hurtful remembrance that would attack my soul, I would say no in the name of Jesus and turn my mind to Him.

I realize that the Lord keeps flowing through my life. There is a Scripture from John 7, where Jesus stood up in the temple and cried out, "If anyone believes in me, out of his innermost heart will flow rivers of living water." (He was speaking of the Spirit, which they hadn't received yet). The Holy Spirit is the presence of God that is always there and always available—even if we don't always feel it. Once we have received and surrendered to the Holy Spirit, – it doesn't go away.

In John 6, Jesus says, "Unless the Father draws him, no one can come to me." It is really the Father who is the drawing power of everything good in this world. So what I say to the Father is, "draw me, I'm in Jesus, and He is in me; with Jesus, draw me to you." Again I turn to Jeremiah "I have loved you with an everlasting love and now in my tender mercy, I draw you to myself." It is all about God drawing us to Himself.

I believe it was Mahatma Ghandi who said if everybody prayed and wanted peace the world would heal, wars would stop. St. Paul talks about the spirits of the air that are always there to descend into the human condition. The devils are there and ready to come into action but more importantly, the angels are too. I think of it like the Internet, everything is stored there, and it is a framework, an actual reality of the presence of God and truth, and evil. It comes into our lives when we call on it or when it is imposed on us as well. So we have to be on guard all the time to stand against the evil that is coming at us and we have to be open to and call upon the presence of God.

Pope Leo the 13th at the end of the 1800's had a vision of what was to come in the 1900's. He sent a prayer out to the whole Catholic Church and I remember praying it as a child: "Saint Michael the Archangel, defend us in battle. Be our protection against the wickedness and snares of the devil; May God rebuke him, we humbly pray; And do thou, O Prince of the Heavenly Host, by the power of God, thrust into hell Satan and all evil spirits who wander through the world for the ruin of souls. Amen."

The angels are given to us as protection by this simple prayer taught to children "Angel of God, my guardian dear. To whom God's love commits me here. Ever this day (night) be at my side to light, to guard, to rule and guide." That prayer tells us the mission of the angels in our lives. The angels are working but are we listening, watching, are we calling on them?

Somewhere along the line, someone told me that we could learn our angel's name by asking for it. So I prayed and heard Hallel, which means praise God. So I call on my guardian angel a lot. He is a messenger and a guard. He will protect and guide me but he is not the spirit of God in me.

This brings me back to the realization that if I have the spirit of God I have everything. If I'm in God I'm in the right place. In Him we live, move and have our very existence. I can't get away from God – He is everywhere I go. I'm not always aware of Him but the reality is that He is there loving me, blessing me. When I call on Him, He is there.

Trust is the bottom line. Jesus said "Trust in God and Trust in me. In my Father's house there are many dwellings." In anticipation of the gift of Himself to us, Jesus promised "On that day you will know that you are in me and I'm in you."

This is eternal life, to know the Father and Jesus Christ whom He had sent. Knowing another person is the most intimate knowledge and love of our heart toward another.

All of this is what keeps me going. It is the pilot light that I turn on again and again. On any given day when I don't feel great, I may get up and make the sign of the cross. Sometimes I wake up and say the Lord's Prayer. Or I wake up and pray the Hail Mary. One day I prayed that Mary would give me another way of saying, "Blessed be the fruit of thy womb Jesus." The word that came to me is "Hail Mary full of grace the Lord is with you, blessed are you among women and glory be Jesus" (acknowledging His resurrection). I actively strive to keep the words of faith flowing through my mind. Sometimes I will say to myself, "I should read scripture more," but I've stored it up in my memory. So in a way I do read scripture as it is an active recall and tape running through my mind and into my life.

The reality is that we are in this world for as long as God wants us to be. I'm in this world to praise the glory of His name. Praying to be able to pray. Praying to be able to live in the faith. Prayer is the most important thing on an active basis in our lives because it implies faith, trust and acknowledgement of who God is and the glory and salvation of God. Prayer is declaring my soul to be at rest and letting God do what He wants to do in my life, on this day, in this hour, in this next moment. Contemplation is letting the presence and word of God accomplish in me at any moment what He wants to do.

Standing against evil in the name of Jesus. Calling upon the person of Jesus to be present. In moments of distress to trust that I will be safe in the presence of Jesus. That all will be well. That is the active thinking of my mind and soul. I am sealed in the Holy Spirit in baptism and marked as Christ's own forever. The indelible mark on the soul of a baby. It is a gift. The community of people who have brought that child to receive the Holy Spirit have also received the Holy Spirit. This is an example of being ambassadors of reconciliation in Christ.

This is the flow of my mind and soul.

Prayers I Repeat to Myself and For Others

Prayers are so important to me and the ones I memorized are so helpful to me because they bring me back into focus.

I pray this several times a day, uniting with priests throughout the world celebrating the Eucharist: Oh Lord, I offer you the body and blood, the soul and divinity of your dearly beloved son, our Lord Jesus Christ, in atonement for my sins and the sins of the world. And I add to it- of my family, my extended family and the many people I've known or worked with over the years. And in thanksgiving for your unending love and generosity.

I often pray this, and teach people to pray this, who are ill:

For the sake of your sorrowful passion, have mercy on me and on the whole world.

Oh God so fill my heart with faith in your love that with calm expectancy I may make room for your power to possess me and gracefully accept your healing through Jesus Christ our Lord. Amen

I learned this years and years ago and I pray it often. It's a good one for Lent:

Soul of Christ sanctify me

Body of Christ save me

Blood of Christ inebriate me

Water from the side of Christ wash me

Passion of Christ strengthen me

Oh Good Jesus hear me

Within your wounds hide me

Permit me not to be separated from you

From the wicked foe defend me

At the hour of death call me

And bid me come to you

That with your saints I may praise you forever and ever. Amen

When I think of those I know who have departed:

Eternal rest grant to her O Lord and let perpetual light shine upon her and may her soul and the soul of all the faithful departed rest in peace.

Salve Regina

Hail, holy Queen, Mother of Mercy,

Hail our life, our sweetness and our hope.

To thee do we cry,

Poor banished children of Eve;

To thee do we send up our sighs,

Mourning and weeping in this valley of tears.

Turn then, most gracious advocate,

Thine eyes of mercy toward us;

And after this our exile,

Show unto us the blessed fruit of thy womb, Jesus.

O clement, O loving,

O sweet Virgin Mary.

Pray for us, O holy Mother of God,

that we may be made worthy of the promises of Christ.

I frequently pray the Our Father, Hail Mary, the Memorare as a way of setting my heart and mind toward God.

I often sing. Barbara and I would sing on the way to church: Praise God in the highest heaven, praise Him on his mighty throne. Praise Him for His wonderful deeds. Praise Him for His sovereign majesty. Alleluia, Alleluia, Alleluia.

In 1982 in Mary's revelations to the kids in Medjugorje, they asked her:

Do many people go directly to Heaven? She answered, not so many

How many go to purgatory? Mostly everyone

How many people go to hell? Many

I think of all the difficulties people have as they grow old, they can take it patiently and use that as a sort of purgatory. Purgatory is a cleansing. When I get impatient I think, oh here I go, help me Lord.

We have to work to go against all those tendencies that are not of God. It's not concentrating on sin, it's more like cleansing the deck, tidying the living room, or cleaning the bathrooms or kitchen. We carry baggage. It's not something I dwell on.

I think when we have difficulties in our life and we try to put God on the front burner in view of people that is a good thing. Sometimes I'm on the phone with someone and I'll be inspired to share things with them.

Prayers can really reveal and fuel our faith.

Conclusion

By saying these prayers and reciting these scriptures I'm able to restart my spiritual engine, my soul.

In churches and religious instruction, we learn a lot about God. But what is important to remember is that knowing about God and knowing Him personally are two different things. John 17 tells us "Eternal life is this: to know you the only true God and Jesus Christ who you have sent." That is a key to reality – to know you, dear God, in the most intimate and loving way through the Holy Spirit. This is what is essential.

Jesus said "Abide in my love," and he gave the basis for that. "As the Father has loved me, so have I loved you. Abide in my love." I put the following Scripture from John 17:26 on my ordination card: "Father I pray that the love You have had for me, may be in them, so that I may be in them."

God is with us and is in us. His presence and abiding love is the deepest fact of our existence. This loving God asks us to stay in, abide in, and hold onto His love.

The goal of our life is to be in a living relationship with God. God is love. He wants us with Him forever. And He wants us more than we want Him.

And Jesus continues in John 6:45 "Everyone who listens to the Father and learns from Him, comes to Me."

And now Lord, what claim do we have on the Father? Can we really claim that promise 'You belong to Me'? Once we have opened our hearts to Jesus and given our life to Him, he claims us as His very own. You belong to Me.

Jesus said "you are in me and I am in you." All of this is the Lord's strong desire to be a vibrant, loving presence within us. And to help us to be a vibrant, loving presence to everyone we meet. When we realize this, we have the potential to 'restart' every healthy relationship with others.

Because of this choice on God's part that we belong to Him, we can live in the promise that Jesus has made to us: 'Whatever you ask the Father in my name I will give you.' I often pray the little prayer from the Episcopal Prayer Book. God wants us to bring restoration and renewal to those who are sick, or have a physical impediment.

"O God, the source of all health: So fill my heart with faith in your love, that with calm expectancy I may make room for your power to possess me, and gracefully accept your healing; through Jesus Christ our Lord. Amen"

In Isaiah, Jesus says "I have loved you with an everlasting love, you are mine."

Jeremiah 29:11 says "for I know the plans I have for you...plans to prosper you and not to harm you, plans to give you hope and a future.

How do we make the claim on God's affection? Because he has first chosen us, before we ever chose Him. He said "I will never leave you nor forsake you."

The whole gospel of St. John is God's urging people to believe in Him. We have all seen the John 3:16 signs at sports stadiums "God so loved the world that He gave his only son that those who believe in Him will live forever." Jesus said "I have come that you may have life to the fullest." His life, his ever recurring new life, propels us into the future of every new day. If we look at Him with an open heart.

I remember the first time I read Acts 17:28 "In Him we live and move and have our very existence." That explanation opened up a new world of understanding to me. God is everywhere all the time, as close as the air we breathe. We can breathe in His new life, continuously, all day long. All the above claims that Jesus made are above and beyond what we can totally absorb but they are true. Because He said it and His words in the Scriptures restate it, again and again. The Scripture says "we see now as in a clouded mirror but then we will see face to face." Many people have retold their experience when seemingly dying that they saw the LIGHT and they realized that it was the brilliant light of Jesus.

When Mary and Joseph found Jesus in the temple, they didn't admonish him but they asked him "why?". He answered "didn't you know I am to be about the business of my Father?" Jesus said to Mary, "if not now, when?" At the marriage feast, when Mary approached Jesus it was a moment of consternation for the hosts. They had run out of wine and people were asking for more. When she directed the servants to "do whatever he tells you" it was her way of asking Jesus to do something. Jesus didn't want to do that miracle because it was the beginning of a whole series of choices. And if He started that chain of miracles, it would only increase the tension with the Jewish leaders. And Mary replied to him, "if not now, when?"

I know who my savior is and I know that He has drawn me to Himself and I am safe in His hands. No matter what. My sinfulness. Lack of faith. Forgetfulness. Broken promises. None of that can separate me from God's love for me and Christ Jesus, my Lord.

I think that God has presented us at times with a situation that is going to challenge us and make us grow. And will draw us closer to him. Some have been pleasant and some have been very hard.

But we are what we are by the grace of God and His grace has not been futile in our lives.

God is much involved in our whole lives, even if we don't see or feel Him. Bidden or not, God is present. This ties right in with St. Paul's "In Him we live, and move and have our very existence". But He doesn't impose, He lets us be free. He allows us to make our own decisions and choices and gradually learn how to love, be generous in our love and to be forgiving. God is involved in the details but He doesn't manipulate them. So understanding His presence and positive involvement in our life; the more we are able to be aware of that then the more we are able to be open to all that he wishes for us.

Life is full of trials and tribulations. In our later life, it is just abandonment to God. I can't do anything Lord, I rely on you completely. Every good you want me to do, you have to prompt me to do. Maybe I have ideas, but I have to test it to see if it is what you want me to do. I have to learn to listen to the Spirit.

Our whole life is meant to be a prayer. But you say, I can't manage that. God says I know you can't.

Mary said God never rejects any heartfelt prayer. Just pray sincerely the way you are able to pray.

Lord, let's create a little deal. When I think of someone would you count that as a prayer? People run through my mind all the time. I do think of and pray for people actively all the time. But when I just think of someone, the Lord will take that as a prayer.

You are such a good and loving father. I can think of you in human reflection in the way God the Father is. Everything that is good and loving in this world is a reflection of God. When Jesus said "God sees the heart." What is he looking for? He is looking for some reflection of Himself in our heart. The real reflection is love. He has to see that there is love in our heart. That is going to be the real test for each of us. The love of God is in our hearts through the Holy Spirit that has been given to us.

Faith is a decision. God wants us to make a decision to just do it. To follow Jesus' words.

When people are intimidated or fearful, I advise them to just love the people they are with. Pour out God's love and move forward.

Through this collection of memories and explanation of faith it is clear that I am not a perfect man. However, I have always tried to pour out God's love to others. And if there is a legacy that I want to impart to everyone that I've known throughout my life, it is that Jesus truly loves us and all we are asked to do is to pour that love out to others. "Go in peace to love and serve the Lord."

A family gathering in Granby, CO in 2010

Barbara and I at our daughter Barrie's wedding 2007

Our grandchildren at a family gathering in Denver 2017

Our family at our Ryan & Jenny's wedding in July 2023 (missing grandsons Harrison & Christian and Hattie born July 2024)

With our youngest grandchild, Hattie Rose, born July 2024